Ferdinand S. Mathews

Familiar Features of the Roadside

The flowers, shrubs, birds, and insects

Ferdinand S. Mathews

Familiar Features of the Roadside
The flowers, shrubs, birds, and insects

ISBN/EAN: 9783337224325

Printed in Europe, USA, Canada, Australia, Japan

Cover: Foto ©Andreas Hilbeck / pixelio.de

More available books at **www.hansebooks.com**

MOUNT WASHINGTON IN SPRING.

The home of the Peabody bird.

FAMILÍAR FEATURES OF THE ROADSIDE

* * *

THE · FLOWERS · SHRUBS
BIRDS · AND · INSECTS

BY

F. SCHUYLER MATHEWS

AUTHOR OF FAMILIAR FLOWERS OF FIELD AND GARDEN, FAMILIAR
TREES AND THEIR LEAVES, THE BEAUTIFUL FLOWER GARDEN, ETC.

WITH ONE HUNDRED AND SIXTY DRAWINGS
BY THE AUTHOR, AND MANY OF THE SONGS
OF OUR COMMON BIRDS AND INSECTS : : : : :

NEW YORK
D. APPLETON AND COMPANY
1897

PREFACE.

It might be possible to find a wider field for the study of Nature than the highway, but in many respects certainly not a better one; for, if we keep on traveling, we will have eventually seen and heard about everything that is worth seeing and hearing in the wide world.

What kind of a country is that without a road? Hardly an interesting or beautiful one, and very probably a barren, trackless waste; certainly not a wilderness, for that, with its wealth of wild life, its solemn forests and majestic mountains, is most frequently the objective point for which the road was built.

The road will lead us everywhere; to the top of the loftiest mountain, to the margin of the sea, across peat bogs, through primeval forests, over green meadows, along ferny pastures, down shady glens, over pleasant hills, beside silvery lakes and gliding, shining rivers, over rushing brooks, and,

finally—we must read the next guideboard, for that
tells where the end is—"To ——town," just the
place we wish to get out of, so we can see something.

Yes, see something else besides brick walls and
stone pavements, and hear something different from
the ceaseless din of the busy, restless town. How
delightful to hear and know the voice of every bird,
and to see and know the face of every flower, as we
pass over the highway which crosses the open fields!
We know the whistle of the locomotive, but we do
not recognize the whistle of the peeping hyla in
spring. We may know the chirp of the English
sparrow, but the voice of the Peabody bird, his
American cousin, is an unfamiliar one. There is
yarrow, tansy, thorn apple, and wild carrot in every
empty lot within the city limits; all these we can
name, although each is a tramp from the old country, but our own dainty pipsissewa and twin flower
are strange, new characters. It is well that there is
much for some of us to learn.

Fortunately, there are extremely few who know
every wild flower and who can name every shrub
by its leaf, and every bird, frog, cricket, and grasshopper by his song. If there were such a man, how
intolerably wise he would be! The world is wide,
and creation is infinite; we should not expect to

know everything under the sun. There is not and there never was a student of Nature so perfectly gifted and equipped that he could master all the branches of his profession. Practical and theoretical knowledge are rarely, if ever, fully and equally developed. The patience and ability to pursue a thoroughly systematical course of investigation is possessed by very few; a penetrative mind may be greatly hampered in the search for truth by an imperfectly developed sense of tone and color. So far as tone and color are concerned, there are very few people, anyway, who can hear and see with *absolute* accuracy. How many are there who, without instrumental aid, can whistle with perfect pitch the key of C? How many can remember a given color and match it by memory months later? Yet the ability to do either of these things unquestionably belongs to the perfectly gifted and equipped student of Nature; but even with this ability, there is still nearly everything for the student to master if he would really know Nature. There are a thousand facts never to be learned from books, which only grassy meadows and dimly lit forests can teach; yet it is quite as true that one may live under the shadow of the forest for a lifetime, and through lack of interest never learn the secret of its hidden life.

So it happens that a fullness of wisdom can never

be possessed by any one individual; as a consequence, complete knowledge accrues through a number of channels each one of which is supplied by some specialist; but the source of all knowledge is Nature. Ours, then, is the boundless opportunity of learning directly from the borders of the road many simple and interesting facts; I say boundless, because the small beginning opens expansively toward a larger study of Nature, which becomes more and more attractive the further we advance.

One of the first things which impresses the observer of Nature is her infinitude. There is a new kind of a bug on some stick or stone in every county we enter. There are countless miniature butterflies (*Hesperia*) flitting among the weeds and grasses, no two of which are alike. A well-known butterfly crosses our path, and scarcely is he gone before two new ones appear, neither of which we can recollect ever having seen before. The tree toad's familiar voice pipes in the swamp, but there are other voices piping with it whose origin we can not trace to their proper source. To every one thing we know, or think we know, there are twenty others which we are quite sure we do not know. A wild rose, we thought, was simply a wild rose; but we learn that there are a dozen species, each one of which has a very distinct character of its own. Eglantine we

thought we knew, but here is a specimen closely
resembling it which proves to be quite a different
flower. The little frog called the Savannah cricket
chirps his cricketlike chirp in New Jersey, and we
imagine we hear him in New Hampshire; but no—it
is another larger frog with a similar voice. We
thought a cricket was simply a cricket with a chirp
the same the world over; not so! there are crickets
and crickets, and each species has it own song. The
whip-poor-will certainly seems to sing the same
familiar old tune North and South; perhaps he does,
but in three or four evenings, after having listened
attentively, we discover that every song is different,
not only in key, but in construction, octaves occurring in some, and thirds or fifths occurring in others.
No two robins sing precisely the same melody; no
two Wilson thrushes roll out their double-toned notes
in exactly the same way.

Always variety, endless variety; never any sense-
less repetition in Nature; she gives us a serial story
which is never fully told. Month succeeds month,
chapter succeeds chapter, and ever there is something
new. The few records contained in the following
pages are only an introduction to a boundless world
whose story would fill a library of astounding magni-
tude! But the little that I have given comes straight
from the country highways and byways, and many

things are drawn beside the pictures of their own homes.

I hope the scraps of music which I have introduced will stimulate a little interest in a somewhat neglected phase of wild life. We certainly have very meager records of bird music, and until the notes of our singing birds are completely and fully recorded, we will never possess a complete knowledge of the birds themselves. However imperfect the average ear is in catching and retaining a musical tone, it is impossible to believe that there are many too dull to distinguish apart the songs of the warbling and the red-eyed vireos. We might as well persuade ourselves that a person with average good eyesight can not tell a square apart from a triangle. I might record a dozen songs of as many red-eyed vireos, and although each would be different from the other, the general principle of *construction* would remain the same in all. A record of the warbling vireo's music would also reveal its individuality. To the unfortunate person who could not read music the difference in the *appearance* of the written music of these two birds would not only be perfectly apparent, but as marked as the difference between a triangle and a square.

I regret that the limits of the book would not enable me to include many other birds, crickets, and frogs; their music is interesting and beautiful; but I had to draw the line somewhere, and as a consequence the bright-winged, sweet-songed redstart, and the graceful, clucking American cuckoo, which, by the way, is not a bit like its European relative, for it does not steal a march on other birds' nests—these fell on the other side of the line!

The record of the music of Swainson's thrush is meager but reliable; that of the hermit thrush does full justice to his musical thirds but not to his brilliant fifths. The song sparrow, with the prominent spot in the middle of his breast which is easily distinguished by the aid of the opera glass, is fairly represented by his music; the other sparrows are legion, and would require a volume for anything like a complete record. One of them, however, is separated from all the rest by the simple and striking character of his song. The white-throated sparrow, or Peabody bird, as he is called, is an extremely interesting little fellow who, if we respond to his call, will follow us for a mile or more, singing from treetop to treetop; and those who are willing to undertake the arduous climb through Tuckerman's Ravine at the foot of Mount Washington for the sake of a charming bit of bird music and grand mountain scenery will be amply repaid for their toilsome jaunt by some of his sweetest melodies.

I desire to express my grateful acknowledgments

to Dr. B. L. Robinson and his assistants, Mr. Fernald and Mr. Greenman, who gave me convenient access to many specimens of the Harvard herbarium; to Mr. Samuel Henshaw of the Agassiz Museum, who provided me with many of the entomological specimens which I have sketched; and to Mr. W. Faxon, without whose advice my bird sketches would have lacked certain important points. I should also explain that the unusual employment of capitals in the specific names of birds, a proceeding contrary to ornithological rule, is due to an effort to maintain consistency throughout the book; as there are more flowers than birds mentioned, it seemed to me advisable to adopt the *botanist's* principle with reference to names.

But after all, "What's in a name?" If the flower and the bird are unmistakably identified, all is properly put. The best thing about the hermit thrush is his inimitable, silvery song; the worst thing about him is his ponderous Latin name! If I could illuminate his music as it deserved, the notes would be of burnished gold set in bars of silver !

F. Schuyler Mathews.

El Fureidis, Blair, Campton, N. H.

CONTENTS.

LIST OF FULL-PAGE ILLUSTRATIONS.

xiii

FAMILIAR
FEATURES OF THE ROADSIDE.

The Pioneer of Spring.—Skunk Cabbage (*Symplocarpus fœtidus*).

CHAPTER I.

EARLY WILD FLOWERS, CATKINS, AND SPRING PEEPERS.

THE borders of the road are like the embroidered margin of a fine garment, full of beautiful and elaborate detail. If I wished within a limited space of time to gather a variety of wild flowers, I should follow the highway and leave rolling meadows and rocky slopes to themselves; for, sooner or later, each condition peculiar to the flower of the hillside, forest,

2   1

field, and swamp I should be sure to encounter in an extended tour along the public road.

Unfortunately, we quite often pass on our way with unobservant eyes. The dandelion spreads its wealth of gold at our feet, and we do not stoop to notice it; probably if this wealthiest of all the golden wild flowers was endowed with a voice, it would reproach us in the words of the prophet, " Is it nothing to you, all ye that pass by ? " And we might have to reply with perfect candor, " Nothing; our world is not a world of dandelions." But if we should pause to examine the wonderful golden flower under a powerful magnifying glass, we might discover a new world of absorbing interest, a very familiar one to our fellow-traveler on the highway, the burly bumblebee; for her,* at least, the dandelion is a mine of wealth, a golden storehouse filled with riches of pollen and nectar!

The dandelion is the richest but not the earliest flower of spring: there are many others which appear on the roadside much earlier. In the cold, wet hollow the ill-scented skunk cabbage (*Symplocarpus fœtidus*) is a pioneer, and long before April it has passed its prime and become unsightly in its miry

---

* The bumblebee of spring is nearly always a " queen."

retreat; in its place the marsh marigold (*Caltha palustris*) appears, a flower with scarcely less gold in its cup than the dandelion possesses. But the earliest wild flower of spring is undoubtedly the hepatica or liverwort (*Hepatica triloba*); this dainty, purplish white flow. er appears before its new leaves (the large purple-blotched ones are last year's; the new ones are tiny and fuzzy) sometime in early April, next to a lingering bit of snow, and among the withered leaves beneath the trees at the woodland border of the road.

Hepatica.

I have found the hepatica in some seasons earlier than the trailing arbutus (*Epigœa repens*), but this is a matter of personal experience. William Hamilton Gibson asserts positively that the flower is really the first to appear, and I believe he is quite right. It is the easiest thing in the world to pass the hepatica without noticing it, so closely does it snuggle among the withered leaves; on this account I am inclined to believe it comes and goes quite undiscovered, while the conspicuous arbutus never fails to attract attention.

The bloodroot (*Sanguinaria Canadensis*) is another early April flower, whose white blossom of poppylike delicacy expands before the leaves; then there is the rue anemone (*Anemonella thalictroides*), whose flowers grow in clusters, and the windflower or wood anemone (*Anemone quinquefolia*),* whose flowers grow singly; both of these appear side by side while the bloodroot is still in blossom. If there is a rocky bank near, here we may also look for the rock flower (*Saxifraga Virginiensis*) with its spikes of small white blossoms. Farther along we will be sure to find the miniature whitlow grass (*Draba verna*), whose four white petals are deeply notched; this is pre-eminently a roadside character; indeed, it is a regular tramp which has crossed the ocean and is apparently still on the way to other parts. This flower blooms as late as May also; we will find it on sandy or waste ground.

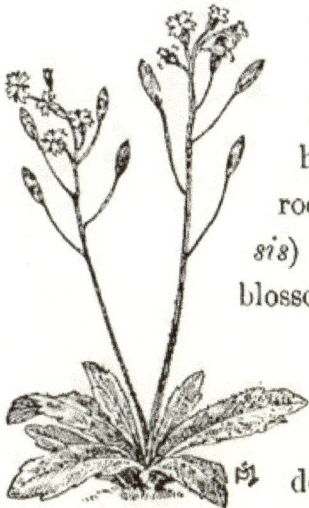

Whitlow Grass.

---

* Also named *Anemone nemorosa*.

It belongs to the Mustard family, which is characterized by four-petaled flowers.

The spring beauty (*Claytonia Virginica*) frequently appears as early as the first of April in southern New England and New
York ; its beautiful, pale,
pink - white blossoms veined
with a deeper pink, are
among our prettiest wild flowers. I should expect to find the
Claytonia, perhaps with a bumblebee visitor tumbling over its
frail petals, in the rich grassy
borders of the road near the
edge of the tiny streamlet
that finds its way to the hollow
where the overflowing brook
hurries along.

I have already alluded to the
bumblebee as " she." As a matter
of fact, in spring these big, golden-
hipped creatures are generally queen
bees searching for pollen and nectar.
The spring beauty is precisely the kind   Spring Beauty.
of a flower which needs the visit of the
bumblebee ; its pistil develops the graceful, curled
tips (which are simply the portals leading to the im-

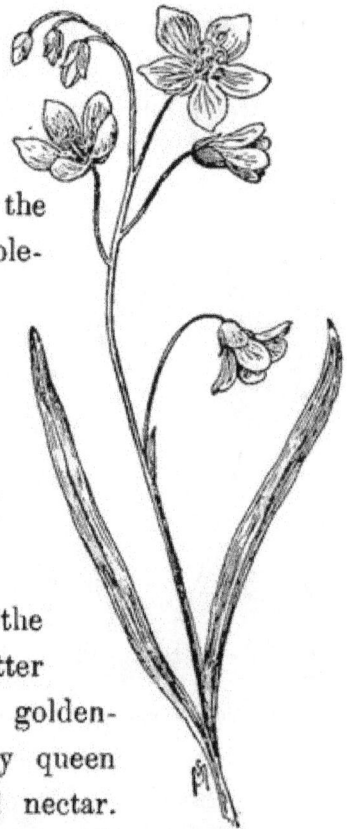

mature seed at the base), too late to receive the pollen from the earlier developed anther! My drawing will show the immature pistil with its "closed doors" at the time the anthers which bear the pollen are ripe, and also the mature split-topped pistil whose open portals are pretty sure to scrape the pollen from the visiting bumblebee's back. The spring beauty is not a self-fertilized plant; Nature has so arranged matters that the bee shall bring the ripened pollen from one flower to the ripened pistil of another.

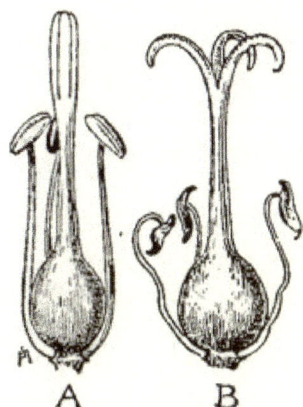

Pistil of Spring Beauty: A, immature; B, mature.

Among the earliest of the violets are the yellow ones. The round-leaved violet (*Viola rotundifolia*) is perhaps the earliest of all, as its tiny blossoms appear in Pennsylvania soon after the snow has gone. This violet grows on the woodland border, and we will find it hugging the damp rich mold, with its roundish leaves flat upon the ground ; in midsummer these leaves are fully two inches in diameter. The flower is pale yellow marked with madder-brown veins. The downy yellow violet (*Viola pubescens*) grows about ten inches high ; the tiny yellow blos-

som is borne on a short stem which issues from between a pair of leaves fully eight inches above the
ground. Both of these flowers bloom sparingly in
early May on the roadsides of the Northern States,
but neither is as common as the blue violet (*Viola
cucullata*), which, on or about
Decoration Day, holds exclusive possession of the cold wet
ground near the spring or the
horse trough.

The daintiest spring flower of
all, I think, is the one which bears
the rather rude but suggestive
name, Dutchman's breeches
(*Dicentra cucullaria*). This
beautiful little plant is frequently to be seen on the
rocky ledges in the valley of
the Hudson River and in the
rich woods westward. It is also

Round-leaved Violet.

common in some parts of Central Park, New York,
and Prospect Park, Brooklyn. The blossom is white
tipped with creamy yellow, and the extremely ornamental foliage is blue-green. Dr. Abbott says : " To
think that such a plant should be called 'Dutchman's
breeches' ! If this abomination were dropped from
Gray's Manual, perhaps in time a decent substitute

would come in use.   But why not call it dicentra?"
I should answer, because to the great majority of
people any name foreign to our language is either

Dutchman's Breeches.

enigmatical or meaningless.   Dutchman's breeches
means something, and it does not seem quite abom-
inable if we look at it from the right point of view.

I like the name because of its Knickerbocker flavor, and although it is suggestive of a bit of rude humor, it is not without a certain poetic significance. The word Dutchman, to be sure, is so loosely used nowadays that it does not suggest much more than the unromantic personality of the prosaic corner grocer, but I have yet to find the American who is ashamed of his Dutch blood! So I do not think we need be ashamed because one of our wild flowers bears the name "Dutchman's breeches." * Breeches, it is true, sounds a bit unrefined, but I insist that it is poetic; substitute the modern " pants " for it, imagine, if possible, Hendrick Hudson clothed in them, and, presto! all the poetry attached to the romantic vigils in the Catskills is gone. There are two flowers which are inseparably associated in my mind with Rip Van Winkle and Hendrick Hudson—one is Dutchman's breeches and the other is Indian pipe; both of them are ghostly white, and both are commonly found in the country of the Dutch settlers. Why not let Dutchman's breeches

---

* That these at least possessed magnificent proportions the following historical incident certainly proves beyond a shadow of doubt: Some Indians were induced by a settler to sell for a small consideration as much of their land as could be bounded by a pair of breeches. To their chagrin the Dutchman cut his ample breeches into narrow strips, and sewing these together formed with them so long a strip that it encompassed several acres!

stand in commemoration of our Dutch ancestors? In early spring the dainty flower lines every wooded bank which slopes toward the Hudson River. A close relative of *Dicentra cucullaria* is another little spring plant called squirrel corn (*Dicentra Canadensis*); this bears little two-spurred, heart - shaped, greenish white flowers tinged with pink, which are sweet - scented. We will find the squirrel corn only on the borders of rich woods in the North; the foliage is like that of its relative, and its roots bear tiny tubers resembling grains of corn (see my sketch of four tubers). It blooms throughout April.

Still another early spring flower is the wild ginger (*Asarum Canadense*). We will find this plant on the edge of the wood that flanks the hillside. The solitary flower is dull madder brown, and is seen close to the ground where the two leafstems rise to the large furry leaves

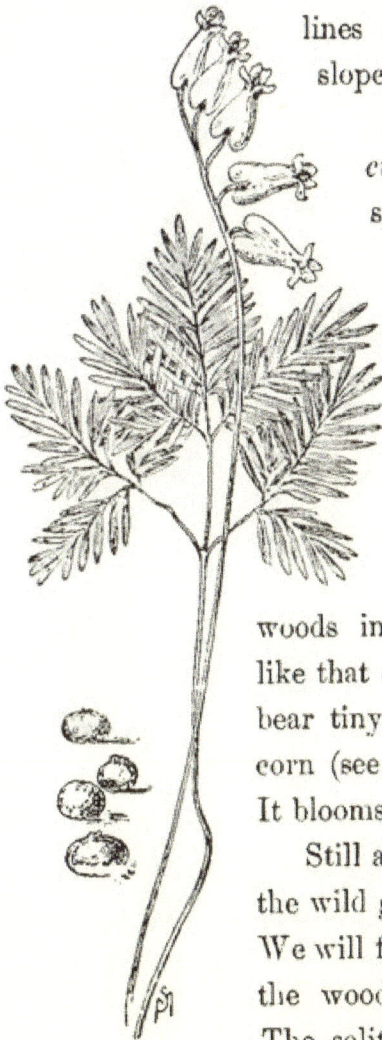

Squirrel Corn.

above which measure four or five inches across; these
are broad, heart-shaped, and more or less pointed.
The Canada wild ginger is quite
common northward; its aromatic, stinging root-
stock has
the flavor
of ginger.
  While
we are yet
passing through the
woodland we will most
likely find another early
flower, the mandrake or
May apple (*Podophyllum
peltatum*); this blooms in
May. The drooping white
flower with half a dozen or
more petals is borne between

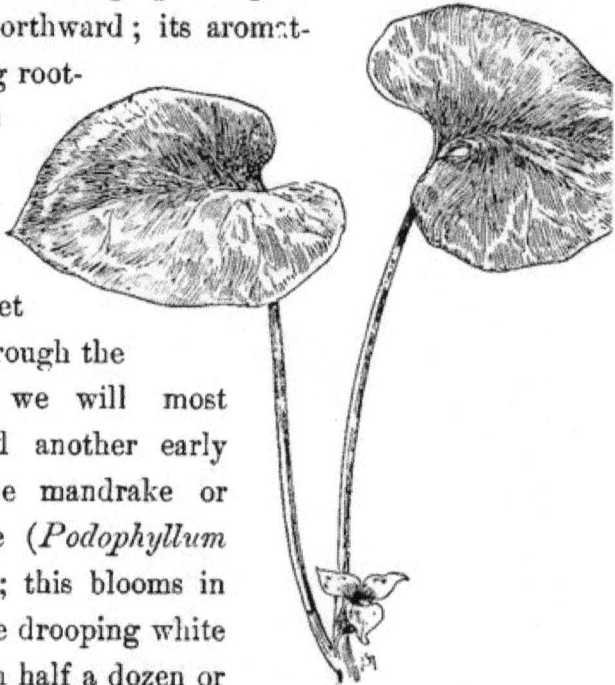

Wild Ginger.

two large leaves which have from five to nine lobes;
the plant has also flowerless stems which bear only
larger leaves supported in the middle like an umbrella. The fruit, which ripens in July and appears
like a tiny lemon an inch and a half long, is edible;
but both leaves and roots are drastic and poisonous—
so says Dr. Gray. As for the fruit, I prefer to let it
alone; it is simply rank!

The most conspicuous flowers which appear on the
roadside in early spring are the alder and willow catkins.   There are two species of alder which are com-

May Apple.

monly found on the borders of swamps and the damp
hollows beside the highway; they flower in early
April before the leaves are well out.   The flowers are

of two kinds,* sterile and fertile ; the former elongated and drooping (a nicely adjusted arrangement
that enables the pollen to drop easily
on the fertile flowers below), and the
latter ovoid or oblong and somewhat
erect. These catkins were formed
in the preceding summer, and
passed through the winter in a
shape resembling a tiny, elongated
green cone ; now they appear in
plumy clusters on the still leafless
branchlets. Should we happen to
jostle the alder bush a cloud of
pollen arises from the sterile flowers, which probably reaches the
fertile ones near by, and thus the
latter become fertilized ; but without doubt a few early bees will
find the pretty ocher-yellow, lav-
ender-brown, and greenish yellow catkins, and these will carry enough pollen on their backs to accomplish what
the pollen cloud left unfinished.

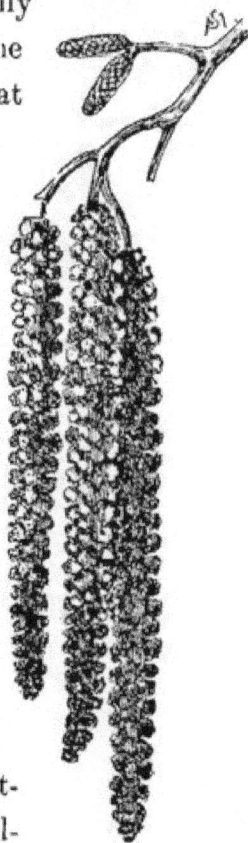

Speckled Alder
Catkins.

The spreckled or hoary alder (*Alnus incana*) is
common northward and westward from Massachu-

* The alders are monœcious; that is, the stamens and pistils
are in separate flowers on the same bush.

setts. This species has broad, oval, dark-green leaves, sharply and irregularly toothed, which are whitish and downy beneath. The smooth alder (*Alnus serrulata*) is found southward and southwestward from Massachusetts; it forms dense thickets in Pennsylvania and Virginia on the borders of swamps, and farther south attains a height of thirty-five feet. The leaves are obovate, and green on both sides; they are usually smooth, but occasionally downy beneath. *Alnus incana* is as common along the roadsides in northern New Hampshire as *Alnus serrulata* is in southern Pennsylvania.

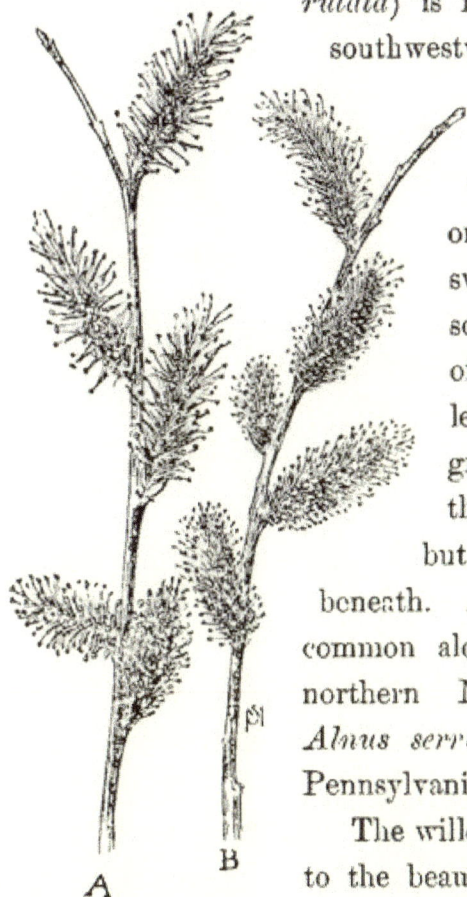

The willows contribute largely to the beauty of the roadside in spring by their beautiful golden-flecked catkins. The glaucous willow (*Salix discolor*) we will always find hanging over the river's brink and the

A

B

Glaucous Willow Catkins: A, sterile flowers; B, fertile flowers.

fence that borders the marshy meadow. The "pussies," about an inch long, appear before the leaves in earliest spring; the sterile and fertile flowers are on separate plants. The catkins, which eventually attain a length of one and a half inches, have brown scales which finally become black; they are clothed with long shiny or silky hairs. The prevailing color of the mature sterile flower is the yellow of the pollen; the fertile flower has a softer, silky appearance, with less of the yellow tone. The leaf at maturity is from two to five inches long and at least one inch

Gray Willow Catkins.

wide, irregularly and somewhat remotely toothed, smooth, and bright green. The glaucous willow grows from eight to fifteen feet high.

The prairie willow (*Salix humilis*) is common on dry and barren ground; the small catkins are from one half to one inch long, and they are frequently bent downward or outward from the branchlets; they appear before the leaves, and are at first silky gray and at last yellowish; the scales are dark brown. The leaf at maturity is from one and a half to three inches long, lance-shaped, without teeth, and the edge is often crinkly or wavy.

This species grows from three to eight feet high.

The dwarf gray willow (*Salix tristis*) is also common on dry ground; the catkins are very small, about half an inch long, globular or ovoid, and loosely flowered. The leaf is one or two inches long, without teeth, and slightly wavy-edged; the leaves are crowded on the branchlets. This species grows from one to one and a half feet high; in general appearance it is grayish, and for that reason is sometimes called "sage willow." It is frequently found in the thickets which border the mountain road.

There are three other willows whose beautiful catkins decorate the highway borders in spring. These are the shining willow (*Salix lucida*), a shrub from six to fifteen feet high, common on the banks of streams; the heart-leaved willow (*Salix cordata*), eight to twenty feet high, usually found in wet situations; and the long-beaked willow (*Salix rostrata*), eight to fifteen feet high, very common on slightly moist ground. The first species (*S. lucida*), has large showy, yellow, sterile catkins, which appear later than the broad, shiny, sharply toothed leaves; the second (*S. cordata*) has beautiful yellow catkins appearing at the sides of the stem with or before the leaves, which are usually heart-shaped at the base; the third (*S. rostrata*) has old-gold-yellow catkins appearing with the leaves, which, when young, are velvety and of a rich olive hue, and fruit capsules tapering to a very long slender beak; this last species is common on both dry and wet ground, while the other two are more frequently found on the borders of swamps.

Now that we are in the vicinity of the catkin-decorated swamp we must not pass it without pausing to listen to the sweet piping voices of the little "peepers" (*Hyla Pickeringii*); these tiny ocher-yellow-brown, smooth-skinned frogs are scarcely an inch long, yet about the first of April, when at five in the afternoon the orchestra is in full chorus, their shrill, ear-piercing notes have no equal in all musical nature, both as to quality and quantity. The first song of spring is either that of the bluebird or Pickering's frog;* it is mere chance which we will hear first. We can scarcely see the little "old-gold" creatures, for only their bulgy eyes and the tips of their noses are above the surface of the pond, and if we approach the margin these instantly disappear. They are not always in the water, though, for we might be fortunate enough to catch a glimpse of one perched on an

---

* The frog called *Acris gryllus* also sings quite as early. According to an old saying, the peepers must be silenced thrice by the frost before the spring weather comes to stay. As a rule, they sing when the mercury stands between 50° and 60°.

inclining weed stem, or seated on the margin among
the leaves and grasses.

I know of no bird except the white-throated sparrow which sings continuously as " high " as Pickering's frog. His song is usually pitched in the key of
F minor, and his note is E slurred to F three octaves
above middle C. Some-
times, however, I detect
other tones pitched low-
er, perhaps in D ; but E
is generally the dominant note, in proof of which I
will give William Hamilton Gibson's concurrent testimony.   He says, " The phee, phee, phee, phee is
uttered in the note E four octaves above middle
C."   But Mr. Gibson would have more correctly
said E in the *fourth octave* above, because the treble
register ends at the *fourth C* above the middle
one.

How phenomenally high both the Peabody bird
and the Pickering's frog sing we quickly learn if we
go to the piano and strike the highest E and B of the
instrument (C is the final note); the bird outstrips
the frog by about four tones and reaches B with apparent ease and undiminished power. After long cultivation I have succeeded in clearly whistling B flat,
but with greatly reduced force; yet these little singers
in the wooded hollow have golden, liquid whistles

THE MEADOWS OF
PLYMOUTH, N. H.

"SPRING PEEPERS,"
HYLA PICKERINGII.

beside which mine is as " sounding brass or a tinkling
cymbal " !

Pickering's hyla leaves the swamp in early July
and is a " tree toad " in autumn ; then his shrill but
less vivacious note is often mistaken for that of a
bird.   He is a great climber ; each of his toes is furnished with a little circular pad by the aid of which he
can hold fast to a slippery surface.   Dr. Abbott gives
a surprising account of the climbing powers of these
tree toads ; I quote what he says : " They are seldom
content with a humble perch, and, when in summer
they quit their aquatic and mud life for an arboreal
one, they often wander to the very highest available
resting places in the trees.   I once found one at the
very top of a tulip tree, at least sixty feet from the
ground."   My drawing of Pickering's frog is accom-
panied by a sketch of a pool near the road which
crosses the Plymouth meadows (Plymouth, N. H.).
In April, about five in the afternoon of a warm day,
this charming bit of meadow road is " set to music "
with the voices of a thousand Pickering's frogs !

There is still another slender, long-legged swamp
singer, called the Savannah cricket (*Acris gryllus*),
who has a modified, rattling whistle.   The Savannah
cricket is about an inch long and green on the back,
with a triangular mark on the head, and on the sides
black edged with cream-color.   These colors some-

times change to extremely pale tints.* The only
"crickets" which I have ever seen, however, were
grass-green and decidedly dark-spotted, with long
narrow heads and prominent eyes. This little frog
also sings in the early spring in the same orchestra
with the other peeper. His tones are not so pure,
though, and they are pitched, I have noticed, in a
lower key; they are loud, but not sufficiently so to
be heard at a great distance. The *Acris gryllus*
has a rattling, cricketlike note,† which can not
possibly be mistaken for the smooth, liquid whistle
of Pickering's hyla. He remains in the high grasses
surrounding the marsh, and
seldom if ever ascends trees.
He is not in New England.

My sketch of the Sleepy
Hollow bridge shows just one of those swampy
spots in which the Savannah cricket finds a spring
retreat exactly suited to his taste. My earliest rec-
ollection of this cricketlike frog is associated with
this old roadway and the grasses and rushes which

---

* Like the chameleon, the tree toad changes color to match its
surroundings, of course as a protection against its enemies. Thus
on a tree trunk the creature will appear brown, but among the
leaves it becomes greenish.

† A note so exactly like that of the cricket that we might think
it was a cricket singing; but the tone is less shrill, more powerful,
and mellow.

SLEEPY HOLLOW, WESTCHESTER
CO., N. Y.

THE SAVANNAH CRICKET,
ACRIS GRYLLUS.

crowd its borders. Here in early spring *Acris gryllus* "crepitates" during the twilight hour to its heart's content; here also, later in the season, the tree toad sings his pathetic, persuasive, "bleating" song—a song which lures one to linger by the old picket fence and recall Irving's story of poor superstitious Ichabod Crane, whose cranium came near being smashed by Brom Bone's terrible pumpkin. We wonder if there were any frogs singing on that eventful autumn evening! I have no doubt whatever that even if the frogs were silent the crickets were not, and certainly *Œcanthus niveus* must have sung if the night were not too cold. Irving records the fact that Ichabod did hear a few midnight notes—"occasionally the chirp of a cricket, or perhaps the guttural twang of a bullfrog" (but this was *Rana Catesbiana*, not our *Acris*) "from a neighboring marsh, . . . and a groan—it was but the rubbing of one huge bough upon another, as they were swayed about by the breeze." Poor Ichabod! I know just how he must have felt, for the rubbing together of two big tree boughs in the forest at nightfall is about the most ghostly, blood-curdling kind of music I know of; it is only to be paralleled by the hollow, grinding, groaning sound of a ferryboat as it clumsily enters the slip.

Sleepy Hollow is quite as quaint and sleepy to-day

as it was years ago when Irving drew its picture with his inimitable pen, and described it as "a little valley or rather lap of land among high hills, which is one of the quietest places in the whole world. A small brook glides through it with just murmur enough to lull one to repose; and the occasional whistle of a quail or tapping of a woodpecker is almost the only sound that ever breaks in upon the uniform tranquillity."

Later in the spring or in early summer we will also hear the crepitating — in plain English, rattling or creaking — notes of the little frog called *Chorophilus trise riatus*; this little fellow never leaves the swamp for the trees,

Chorophilus triseriatus.

and he continues his song throughout the summer. We can not fail to recognize it if by any good chance we can gain the edge of the marsh where we may hear one singer's voice well separated from the general chorus. It has a rising inflection, a moderate crescendo, and a limited range, thus:

The quality of the tones can not be conveyed by note; I might compare it to the scraping of the teeth of a comb, one end of which is wide and the other narrow—a comb, in fact, shaped like the steel one in a music box. The notes are not whistled, and they are therefore entirely unlike those of Pickering's hyla; they are also not vivacious and shrill, but, on the contrary, moderate and soothing. The song of this frog must not be confused with that of the tree toad (*Hyla versicolor*) which we hear in early summer; but of the tree toad's notes I will have something to say further on.

The *Chorophilus triseriatus* is about an inch long; he has slender limbs and toes, and a light ash-gray body striped brown; his skin beneath is yellow-white and somewhat granular; in fact, he is *not* a smooth frog in appearance or in voice! This species is common in the Northwest and in the swampy barrens of southwestern New Jersey. Mr. E. D. Cope has also found it in Gloucester County, N. J., and I am quite sure I have heard it in Monmouth County; but I do not recollect having heard its *unmistakable crescendo* tones in New England. Like the *Acris* and Pickering's hyla, it sings in the latter part of March or early April, but it continues through the spring and early summer, and sometimes it can be heard in the warmest part of the day.

Yet another musical but somewhat harsh note comes to our ears from the marsh in early April; it is that of the wood frog (*Rana sylvatica*), who is brown-yellow tan color, except under the eye, where there is a black streak. This frog is about two inches long. He lives in the woods throughout the summer, and rarely, if ever, visits the water at that time ; but during the breeding season, about the middle of April when

Wood Frog.

the weather is warm, the wooded margin of the pond will resound with the spasmodic, hoarse, clucking notes of this sylvan character—for he really prefers the wood to the water. *Rana sylvatica* is common from Maine to Ohio and Michigan.

CHAPTER II.

On the banks of the stream along which the road follows appear, in April or May, inconspicuous clusters of greenish flowers on the yet leafless, brown, prickly branchlets of the toothache tree (*Xanthoxylum Americanum*). This is a shrub from four to twelve feet high, bearing compound leaves of from five to nine leaflets (usually seven), which are almost if not entirely without teeth, downy when young, but growing smooth. All parts of the tree are pungent and aromatic; if the leaves are crushed they yield a strong lemonlike * odor; this is also very strong in the fleshy fruit, which is about the size and shape of peppercorns. The toothache tree is frequently seen in cultivation; it is supposed to furnish an excellent remedy for toothache and neuralgia.

A near relative of the toothache tree, the three-leaved hop tree (*Ptelea trifoliata*), will be found on

---

* An odor similar to that of the lemon verbena.

rocky roadsides in Pennsylvania, on Long Island, and in the West as far as Minnesota. This shrub, from six to eight feet high, bears on the tips of its branchlets clusters of rather unpleasantly scented, four- to five-petaled greenish white flowers in early June. The leaf is composed of three leaflets without teeth. The hop tree is very beautiful in spring when in bloom, and in the fall its large clusters of decorative, hoplike fruit make it a charmingly ornamental shrub; it is closely related to the ailantus, a fact not difficult to realize after one has noticed the disagreeable odor of the blossoms;

Hop Tree: fruit at A.

but, notwithstanding this slight drawback, the hop tree is decorative and deserving of wide cultivation.

In June we will also see the pretty upright greenish yellow flower clusters of the mountain maple (*Acer spicatum*) on the tall, branching, slender, greenish stems of this shrub, whose dainty, drooping, sharp-pointed leaves are invariably outlined in high relief against the shaded roadside borders of late spring. The mountain maple rarely grows over fifteen feet high.

Another shrub with three leaflets like the hop tree is the bladder nut (*Staphylea trifolia*). This is commonly seen on the roadside, especially among the thickets which border the bog. Its pretty white flowers which terminate the slender branchlets in drooping clusters appear in May. The leaflets (sometimes there are five) are toothed, and the main stems of the compound leaves grow opposite to each other. The bladder nut is a handsome shrub, from six to ten feet high, with green-striped branches, and

Mountain Maple.

Bladder Nut.

(in late summer) extraordinary inflated seed pods like my sketch, which are three-sided and three-celled, each cell containing about three smooth hard seeds. The pod, if crushed, smells like a pea pod.

A most remarkable little ruddy blossom is that which we find on the sweet-scented shrub or Carolina allspice (*Calycanthus lævigatus*) from May to August. Under our nose and with our eyes shut we would imagine the flower was a luscious ripe strawberry, so nearly does it simulate the fragrance of this fruit. The flow-

Carolina Allspice.

ers, which grow singly in the axils of the leaves, must be crushed to yield the odor. *C. floridus* is a species in common cultivation which we will see in parks and gardens ; the other species is found in the mountains of Franklin County, Pa., and southward along the Alleghanies. The leaves are without teeth, oblong, pointed, and bright green. Both bark and foliage are aromatic. The *Calycanthus* will be seen in Prospect Park, Brooklyn, and in Central Park, New York.

A marked feature of the shady roadside in June is the white, flat-topped, and loose flower cluster of the dogwood. There are several species, no one of which should be confused with the so-called poison dogwood (*Rhus venenata*) * belonging to quite a different family (Cashew), which includes the sumachs. The true dogwoods of the family *Cornaceæ* are *not* poisonous. The handsomest member of the group is the flowering dogwood (*Cornus florida*), which bears a large flower with four notched, petallike, showy white leaflets set around the tiny greenish florets. The flowers appear in May before the

Flowering Dogwood.

leaves are fully out; they are succeeded in the fall by small bunches of bright-red, oval berries. This species differs from the others in *not* having a flat panicle of small blossoms; it grows at least twelve feet high.

The very opposite in character of growth from the preceding is the little dwarf cornel or bunchberry (*C. Canadensis*); this tiny plant creeps along

* See page 176.

the damp, wooded roadside of the mountains, and spreads its light-green leaves scarcely five inches above the ground. The white flowers appear in June, and the beautiful bunches of bright scarlet berries are ripe in the latter part of August.

C. alternifolia is a shrub at least six feet high, whose leaves are an exception to the rule respecting their manner of growth; they arrange themselves *alternately* about the tips of the branchlets. The flowers, which appear in May or June, are in flat, open clusters; they are succeeded in late August by blue-black, round, berrylike fruit, which terminates the pretty coral-red, branching stems.

Cornus alternifolia.

C. sericea (called kinnikinic) is a shrub three or more feet high, bearing flat, open flower clusters in June. The silky, downy branches are purplish; the young ones reddish. This species is common in swampy places; the berry is also dark blue.

C. stolonifera is low, from three to four or sometimes six feet high. It is remarkable for its smooth ruddy stems, which by the middle of winter are *blood-red*, and furnish a remarkable bit of color on the borders of the snow-covered meadow. The flower clusters, which are small and flat, appear in June; they are followed in August by whitish or leaden-gray fruit. This species is common in wet places throughout the North.

Cornus sericea.

C. asperifolia is also but three or four feet high, and bears flowers in a similar small, flat cluster, succeeded by a whitish fruit. The branches of this species are brown and rough downy; the leaves are also downy. *C. asperifolia* is a distinctively *Western* species extending from the northern shore of Lake Erie to Minnesota; it also grows in the South.

C. paniculata is a much-branched shrub from four to eight feet high, which bears flowers in numerous loose, almost cone-shaped clusters in May or June. The fruit is white, borne on a pale-red stem; it appears in late August. This species is very common

along the road, beside the river, and in meadow borders throughout the North. The dogwoods all have
ovate-pointed leaves, variable in size, with long veins
which run almost parallel with the edge which is devoid of teeth. In the case of *C. sericea* and *C. asperifolia* the leaves are *downy* beneath, but in the other
species they are *smooth* through-
out; *C. alternifolia*, however, is
minutely downy. These
shrubs are commonly
found beside the high-
way, particularly where it
crosses some thicket - bordered stream. They are extremely beautiful in late
spring when their thin foliage furnishes the most delicate, sober green which we
can find during that season;
and in late summer their
handsome berries, many of
them ruddy stemmed, con-
tribute some of the prettiest

Cornus paniculata.

bits of color which enliven the shaded depths of the
woodland. At this time we may catch a glimpse of
the purple finch and the red-eyed vireo, who venture
down from the tree-tops to feed on the berries which

they so greatly relish; in fact, if we approach a large clump of the alternate-leaved dogwood with caution, we may see a number of our feathered friends pecking at the dark-blue berries, but not at *any* hour of the day; it is early morning when the birds are most hungry, and break-
fast with them is the all - important meal of the day.

From May until July the flowers of the common elder (*Sambucus Canadensis*) are in bloom; but this familiar shrub needs no description ; its c o m p o u n d leaves and hand-some, broad, white flower clus-ters, sweet with

Red-berried Elder: portion of fruit cluster at A.

perfume, are known to us all. Two marked characteristics of the elder are the rank smell of the leaves when crushed and the thick-jointed branches; the latter, when new, are bright green. The large, heavy

4

bunches of purple-black berries, ripe in August, are used for making a medicinal elder-berry wine.

Still another species, the red-berried elder (*Sambucus racemosa*), is common beside the road. The flowers, clustered in a pyramidal panicle, appear in May. The leaves usually have five leaflets. The fruit is ripe in June; in color effect it is one of the most striking and beautiful bits of decoration which the woodland border presents to the eye in early summer. The tiny berries are translucent red, and grouped in effective clusters among the ornamental dark-green leaves. This species grows from two to twelve feet high; the common elder is rarely over ten feet high. I am surprised to note that in the Field, Forest, and Garden Botany Gray calls the flowers of the elder scentless; if one should apply the nose to a good, spreading cluster of the blossoms, I think the experiment would furnish an all-sufficient proof to the contrary. The common elder is a familiar object along the roads of central New Hampshire, and it is quite as familiar to those who pass over the roads in southern New York. The red-berried elder is rather rare in northern New Hampshire.

Succeeding the elders in order come the *Viburnums*, low, straggling shrubs only occasionally found beside the road. One of the commonest of these, dockmackie (*Viburnum acerifolium*), is confined to cool rocky woods; its flat, white flower clusters appear in May or June. The leaves are like those of the maple in shape, and the blackish fruit, about as large as a huckleberry, is ripe in early autumn; it is not fit to eat. Another species, arrowwood (*Viburnum dentatum*), generally found in damp places throughout the North

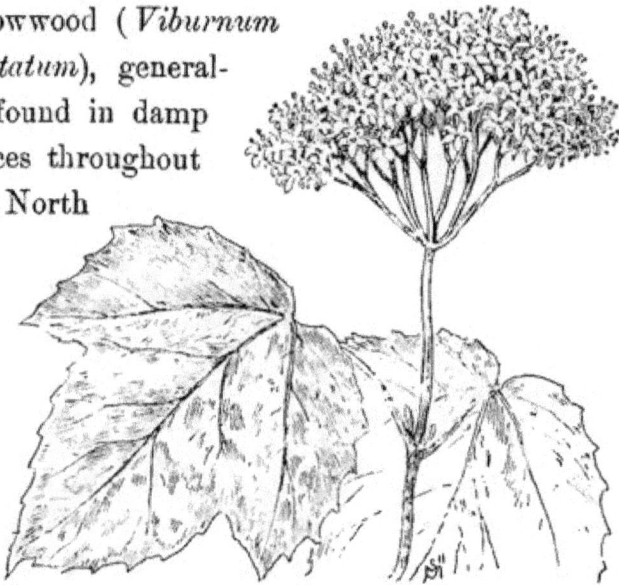

Dockmackie.

and West, has roundish leaves, straight-veined and coarsely toothed, and bears small clusters of white flowers which appear in June. This shrub grows from five to fifteen feet high, and sends out remarkably straight shoots. It is occasionally found in the thickets of the roadside.

On the mountain road which passes through the woods we will probably see the large, almost heart-

shaped, coarse, light-green leaves of the hobblebush
(*Viburnum lantanoides*).   The flat, white flower
cluster appears in May, and the small, hard, red
berries are ripe in September.   This reclining shrub
frequently takes root at the ends of its branches, and
thus trips up the unwary traveler.   It is extremely
common in the White Mountains, along the paths
which wind through the woods in the vicinity of the
Flume House, Franconia Notch, and the Crawford
House, White Mountain Notch, and it can often be
found at an altitude of three thousand feet on the
mountains.

Probably we will see in May or June, on the
woodland road farther south, the insignificant greenish yellow flowers of the fly honeysuckle (*Lonicera
ciliata*).   These grow in twos at the junction of the
leaves with the main stem of the straggling plant.
The leaves are oval or variable in shape, and finely
fringed at the edge.   A near relative of the fly
honeysuckle, a shrub quite common on the wooded
roadsides of the North, is the bush honeysuckle (*Dier-
villa trifida*).   This has small, honey-yellow, or
greenish yellow flowers, usually three on a stalk,
which also grow out from the main stem directly at
its junction with the leafstem.   They bloom from
June to August.   The opposite-growing, sharp-
pointed leaves are toothed.

One of the commonest roadside shrubs of the north country is the buttonbush (*Cephalanthus occidentalis*). Its decorative, spherical heads of yellowish white flowers with long styles are quite an inch in diameter; the strongly veined, blunt, egg-shaped leaves are without teeth. The flowers, however, are late in blooming; they do not appear until late in June or early in July. This shrub grows about four feet high, and is most frequently found on the borders of swamps and streams.

Buttonbush.

The buttonbush thicket is a favorite haunt of the red-winged blackbird (*Agelaius phœniceus*); here the bird finds a safe retreat, seldom molested by enemies; the environment is entirely too aquatic for all visitors other than batrachians. I have no doubt whatever that madame, as she settles on her nest at sundown,

is frequently serenaded by the crepitating, bleating, lullaby notes of the familiar tree toad (*Hyla versi-*

The Red-winged Blackbird.

color), or, should she build her nest in late April, by the more musical but pathetic voices of the spring peepers (*Hyla Pickeringii*). The blackbird is a much slandered but interesting character. Wilson says he has a reputation of being a notorious corn thief, a plunderer of honest farmers; but he proves by careful computation that the farmers are indebted to the birds for destroying an inestimable number of injurious insects. He has calculated that all the blackbirds in the United States during one season of the space of four months eat up sixteen billions two hundred millions of grubs and larvæ! Now, what more could a farmer ask of one family of birds?

If we approach a thicket of alders or button bushes in May (the nesting season) most likely we will see the male bird flirting about in and out among the leaves in evident alarm. He is a handsome creature, nearly ten inches long, dressed in a glossy uniform of black, with deep-red epaulets bordered with buff; his bill is black and very sharp. He is by no means a singer, but, on the contrary, gives expression to his feelings in a variety of confused, rasping, unmusical tones, resembling those of the blue jay; his commonest note sounds like *quonk-a-ree*. If we can recall the shrill squeak of a saw being filed, combined with a turkey-goblerlike sound resembling *jeer-a-rup*, *jeer-a-rup*, we will have the exact counterpart of another of the blackbird's notes—and the jay bird's as well.

In April or early May, on the road which winds through the dark woods, we will possibly see the spice or Benjamin bush (*Lindera benzoin*) in full bloom. The honey-yellow flowers (four to five in cluster) are inconspicuous and tiny; they are grouped in yet larger clusters along the slender branchlets which are as yet bare of leaves; these are alternate-growing, nearly smooth, oval, pointed, and without teeth. The red berries are obovate, and spicy in smell and taste; they have been used in place of allspice. The aromatic odor of the crushed leaves resembles that of gum benzoin. This shrub grows from six to fifteen feet high.

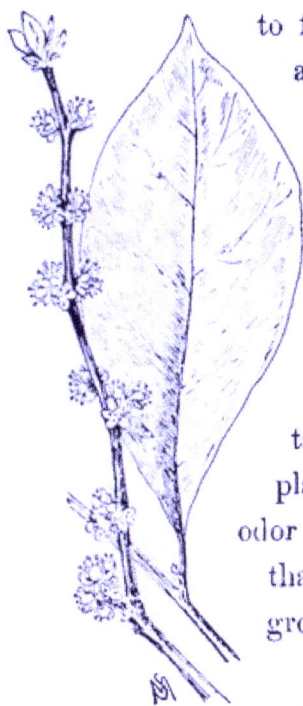

Spice Bush.

Along the roads near the coast, in sandy soil, grows a low shrub from two to three feet, or rarely eight feet, high, called bayberry or wax myrtle (*Myrica cerifera*). This is very common on the island of Nantucket, along the south shore and in the vicinity of Siasconset. The flowers appear in May along with the leaves; the sterile ones, erect and oblong, less than an inch long, and the fertile ones in egg-shaped clusters; the two kinds are mostly on separate plants. The leaves are extremely aromatic when crushed; they are deep olive-green. The small bony nuts, an eighth of an inch in diameter, at first greenish and finally grayish, are incrusted with wax. It was a common practice some years ago for the country people to gather the berries, boil them, and collect the wax by skimming the water.* With this so-called "bayberry tallow" candles and even soap were manufactured. The wax myrtle is found from Maine to Florida; it is also on the shores of Lake Erie.

On the borders of ponds, and perhaps on the roadside adjoining the cold bogs in the North, we will find the

Bayberry,
and leaf of Sweet Gale at A.

---

* In Nova Scotia the wax is extensively used instead of tallow, or is mixed with tallow, to make candles. It has also been mixed with beeswax for the same purpose. Candles made of it diffuse a very agreeable perfume, but give a less brilliant light than those made entirely of animal substance.—*George B. Emerson.*

sweet gale (*Myrica Gale*), another similar fragrant
shrub, which grows from three to five feet high.
The blunt extremities of the leaves are toothed, and
the flowers, similar to those of the foregoing species,
appear in May; the sterile ones are closely clustered.
The little nuts are round and
dotted, and are winged by
a pair of egg-shaped
scales; they are
crowded together
two to six in a
cluster. Sweet gale
is distributed from
Maine westward
along the Great

Sweet Fern.

Lakes to Minnesota,
and southward along the mountains to Virginia.

Sweet fern (*Myrica asplenifolia*), which is, of
course, not a fern at all but another member of the
Sweet Gale family, is common on every pasture and
rocky hill throughout the North. It is unnecessary
to describe it in detail, so well is it known. The
brownish yellow flowers which appear in April or
May are of two kinds on the same plant; the sterile
ones are about an inch long, catkinlike, drooping or
erect, and crowded toward the tips of the branches;
the fertile ones are oblong, one third of an inch long,

and are in rounded clusters with the seed cases surrounded by eight narrow persistent scales, which
grow long and burry as the fruit develops.   The

A road in Buck's Co., Pennsylvania. Sassafras Trees.

fruit, ripe in early July, is a small nut in brown-
green clusters of a burlike appearance.   This
aromatic shrub grows from one to two feet high.

Sweet fern and sassafras, frequently found growing together on the borders of the road, are two
remarkably decorative plants with extremely conventional foliage.

CHAPTER III.

SEVERAL important and interesting members of
the beautiful Rose family are always present in the
mass of shrubbery bordering the country highways
and byways, and these are best introduced in a com-
prehensive group which will aid us in tracing the
general family resemblance.

I call the Rose family a beautiful one because it
not only includes the queen of flowers, but the fruit
trees, spiræas, brambles, whitethorns, shad bush,
mountain ash, and *Pyrus Japonica*, nearly all of
which bear exceedingly handsome blossoms and
fruit.

The distinguishing points of the family are these :
the leaves grow alternately on the branchlets ; the
flowers are regular—that is, they are uniform in
structure ; the petals and sepals are equal in number,
usually there are five of each, and the innumerable
unconnected stamens are a prominent feature in the

44

general color and effect of the blossom. The Rose family is separated into three distinct divisions : these are the Almond or Plum, the Rose, and the Pear sub-families.

Belonging to the first subfamily (Plum) are a few very familiar roadside characters : the first of these is the common wild plum (*Prunus Americana*). Near some old farmhouse one is pretty sure to find this small tree in a neglected condition among the wild shrubbery. It bears its white flowers and dull-green leaves simultaneously in early spring ; the orange-red translucent fruit, about the size of a large cherry, is ripe in early September. The skin is tough but the flavor is pleasant. The tree is scarcely fifteen feet high, and is picturesque to the last degree in either blossom or fruit ; its thorny and scraggy character is quite in keeping with the air of desertion attached to the weather-stained lonely old house near by. On the road which winds about the southern slopes of Mt. Prospect, in the township of Holderness, N. H., there is just such a picturesque abandoned, farm-house, with its cluster of wild plum trees near by, which is as beautiful in May as it is in late August. In blossom or in fruit the tree is always a striking subject for the artist's pencil.

Beside the road not far from the sea a spreading shrub, usually two or three feet high, which bears fruit resembling the wild plum, is frequently seen; this is the beach plum (*Prunus maritima*). It is a straggling bush which flourishes in the sand of the seashore and bears dull-red, tough-skinned, sour fruit fit only for preserving. The white flowers appear before the leaves; these are thick, veiny, and sharply toothed when mature.   Another species closely related to the beach plum is the dwarf or sand cherry (*Prunus pumila*).   But this is generally found on sandy river banks, or in rocky, sandy places along the coast.   The flowers are small and grow in clusters of from two to four; they appear just after the leaves, which are thick, light-colored beneath, shaped somewhat like willow leaves, and toothed near the apex.   The fruit ripens in August, it is very dark red or black, about the size of a wild cherry, and sour or else insipid.   This cherry is found as far West and South as Kansas and Virginia.   It is quite common on the banks of the Pemigewasset and Merrimac Rivers, New Hampshire.

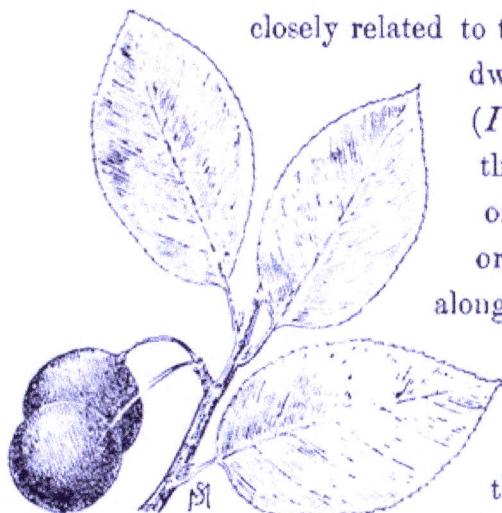

Beach Plum.

The most familiar shrub of our Northern roadsides is the common choke cherry (*Prunus Virginiana*). This is usually not over five feet high, although in some localities it attains the proportions of a good-sized tree. Its leaf is abruptly pointed, and it is usually broadest just beyond the middle; in other words, it is reverse egg-shaped; both leaf and branch when bruised are not very agreeably odorous. In early May its beautiful tassels of white flowers ap- pear, and these in late July are suc- ceeded by clusters of red berries almost as bright as currents; by the end of August the red has turned to black, and the cher- ries are ripe. If one does not mind having the mouth puckered so it becomes difficult to speak, I presume this fruit may be con-

Sand Cherry.

sidered edible; but I prefer to leave it for the birds. I suppose tons of these ber- ries are produced every season on the intervales and roadsides beneath the giant hills of New Hamp- shire; they cling to the bushes, too, until quite late in the fall; it is scarcely strange, therefore, that

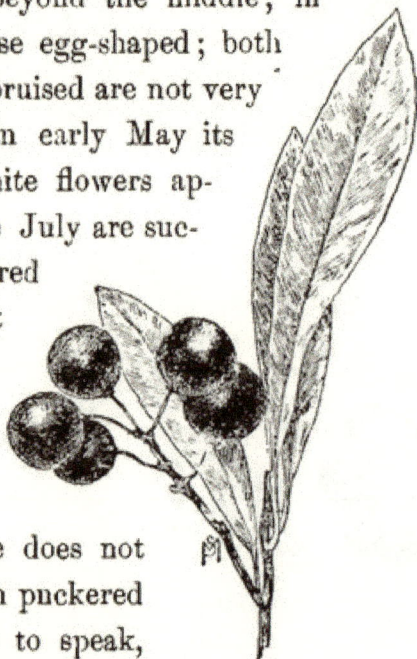

one may find in midwinter among the mountains numbers of our common birds who evidently take the chances of freezing where food is so plentiful. The choke cherries tempt the birds to make a late stay in the autumn; then, when choke, black, and bird or red cherries are all gone, the red winter fruits, wintergreen and partridge berries, still remain scattered over the woodland floors and about the clearings, so the birds stay.

In the Adirondack woods also there is no end of food for the birds; here we will find the black alder (*Ilex verticillata*), smooth winterberry (*Ilex lævigata*), mountain holly (*Nemopanthes fascicularis*), partridge berry (*Mitchella repens*), wintergreen (*Gaultheria procumbens*), creeping snowberry (*Chiogenes serpyllifolia*), and bearberry (*Arctostaphylos Uva-Ursi*). These, and many other seeds and berries too numerous to mention, are plentifully scattered through the Northern forests and clearings, and as late as the end of winter there is still food enough left to keep bevies of birds from starvation. It should not be forgotten, too, that the birds relish the seeds of the coniferous trees, and when the forest floor is hidden with snow the pine-tree cones furnish small granaries for them.

The second subfamily (Rose) consists entirely of shrubs or herbs. It is an interesting division because it reveals several relatives of the queen of flowers not ordinarily recognized as such. The first of these is the beautiful meadowsweet (*Spiræa salicifolia*), which grows from two to three feet high, and adorns every roadside throughout June with its soft clusters of pinkish, flesh-colored flowers. It is a light-green, bushy shrub, with *smooth* stems and double - toothed leaves, which is readily distinguished from hardhack (*Spiræa tomentosa*), as the latter has a *cottony* stem and *deep*-pink flowers. Hardhack also has a pointed flower cluster, which gave rise to its other common name, steeple bush. The shrub called queen of the prairie (*Spiræa lobata*) is a species which is common on the meadows and prairies of the West; it is also cultivated. The handsome plumes of flowers are deep flesh-pink, and the leaves are compound— that is, the leaflets are arranged

Meadowsweet.

on either side of a single stem, like those of the

5

sumach.   This spiræa grows from two to five, or sometimes eight, feet high; the bruised foliage has the odor of sweet birch.

Two members of the Rose subfamily, which are very common indeed in the grassy levels between the shrubbery, are the wild cinquefoil (*Potentilla Canadensis*), a little yellow buttercup-shaped flower, with

Graylock from Chesterfield, Mass.

leaves like those of the strawberry (except that there are five instead of three leaflets), and the strawberry itself (*Fragaria Virginiana*); both are very plentiful on the green-bordered roads about Chesterfield, Mass.

Next we come to the bramble tribe of the Rose subfamily, one of the most beautiful members of which is the purple-flowering raspberry (*Rubus odoratus*).   It has a handsome three-lobed leaf, not unlike that of the maple, and a crimson-pink blossom very similar to a wild rose; unfortunately, the flower at maturity turns a homely, pale magenta, but *never purple.* The fruit of this shrubby plant is like a flat raspberry, with little or no flavor; the long stems are hairy-bristly, not thorny.

The wild red raspberry (*Rubus strigosus*) is thickly distributed over the country from Labrador southward to New Jersey and the mountains of North Carolina, and westward to Minnesota and Missouri. It occupies the roadsides in some localities in New York and New England for miles together; and in many of the old pasture lands of the White Mountain region it grows so luxuriantly, together with the

Wild Red Raspberry.

high-bush blackberry, that it forms almost impassable thickets. The thorny canes, however, are not nearly so murderous as those of the blackberry, and if one is not afraid of a few scratches, a day's "raspberrying" in July, when the season is good, will result in a heaping eight-quart pail of fruit which, in my esti-

mation, equals in flavor the cultivated and much-
prized Cuthbert,* of which our wild berry is the
parent. I find that the birds, especially the sparrows,
indigo buntings, yellowbirds, and chickadees, are
especially fond of raspberries, and at no time can I
enter a broad patch without stirring up a score or so
of little fellows, who do not leave the spot until they
have feasted to complete satiation.

Among the blossoms which afford the best-flavored
honey for the bee, those of the raspberry rank higher
than white clover. In the valley of the Hudson
River, where raspberries are extensively cultivated,
in early morning, during the period of blossoming,
the whitened patches are fairly resonant with the
hum of a million busy bees who leave everything else,
even the earliest and the sweetest of the garden
flowers, for the coveted sweets of the very ordinary-
looking raspberry blossom. Not the sweetest flowers
are always sought by the bee, far from it; for, although white clover and orange blossoms afford much
honey, the trailing arbutus, with its delicate muscatel
odor, is said by apiarists to be quite honeyless,† while

---

* I believe the Cuthbert is a cross between the foreign berry,
called Antwerp, and our own *Rubus strigosus*. The Turner is also
an improved form of *R. strigosus*.

† Not in my opinion, however, as I am quite sure of having
tasted the sweetness in the blossoms. I certainly have concurrent
testimony from Mr. Clarence M. Weed, who records the fact that

such strange flowers as catnip, mustard, hoarhound, melilot, and delphinium are good honey bearers. Of course, apple blossoms, and, in fact, all fruit-tree blossoms, are especially attractive to the bees, the crab apple in particular; but the flowers of the linden, red maple, sugar maple, elm, locust, yellowwood, and tulip trees are equally sought by the bees.

The black raspberry, sometimes called thimbleberry (*Rubus occidentalis*), is also frequently found beside the road. The leaflets are mostly in *threes*, whereas in the red

The High Blackberry.

raspberry they generally occur in *fives*; there is, besides, a characteristic bloom like that on a plum, which covers the canes and the smallest stems. The

the ants, who are always wandering about in search of food, may often be seen trying to get at the nectar in the bottom of the arbutus blossoms. See Popular Science Monthly, May, 1801.

black raspberry is most common in its wild state northward.

The high blackberry (*Rubus villosus*) is another distinctive roadside character in the North. It grows from two to seven feet high, and is armed with recurved thorns stout enough to tear anything but a leathern suit into shreds. The blossoms are narrow-petaled, but large and white as well as beautiful; indeed, a full-flowered spray of blackberry is as picturesque a bit of roadside embroidery as one may well find. The berries themselves in their red and black aspects are inimitably decorative, and the strongly modeled, deep-veined, sharp-toothed leaves are as conventional in arrangement as anything of the leaf kind we can find in Nature.

The blackberry is well named, for it is the most obviously black thing in all the world of flowers and fruit. But *is* it truly black? So far as effect is concerned I must answer yes; but considering it in the light of principle I must answer no; for black hardly has an existence in Nature! To prove this, crush the skin of a blackberry or the petal of a black pansy, and examine the juice under a magnifying glass; there is no black there, but *color*; and as we all know black is the absence of color the proof is conclusive.

The low blackberry, or dewberry (*Rubus Cana-*

densis), may be easily distinguished from the high blackberry by the following characteristics: It is vinelike, long-trailing, and only slightly prickly; it has from three to seven double-toothed leaflets, which are small and nearly, if not quite, smooth in texture, and it is commonest in rocky or sandy soil. The berry has also fewer grains, is more nearly round than that of the other species, and ripens earlier.

CHAPTER IV.

CLOSELY related to the brambles are the dainty
wild roses,* seven species of which are locally distributed along our roadsides from Maine to Minnesota. The most famous wild rose of the country is
the prairie rose (*Rosa setigera*); it grows only in the
West and South. This is a tall, climbing species
armed with nearly straight, large thorns; the leaflets

---

* As far as I could do so, I have avoided straight botanical
descriptions, yet have followed very closely Gray's records of the
salient points of each species, believing that these are the most
useful means for the identification of a rose. The few botanical
technicalities which occur I will explain thus: We should properly look at a leaf point up and stem down, just as we should
naturally look at an egg with the large end down; an *obovate* leaf
is therefore wide end up, and of course stem end down. The
sepal of a flower is *usually* green and leaflike; in the case of the
rose it enfolds the bud and finally withers away on the upper end
of the seed receptacle. The *stipule* of the leaf is that flaring
edge or leaflike formation of the leafstem next adjoining the
branch. It is necessary to understand these simple terms as they
bear directly upon the characteristic differences of species.

SANKATY HEAD LIGHT,
NANTUCKET,
MASS.

are egg-shaped, sharply toothed, and are arranged
from three to five on a stem. The flowers, which
bloom in July, are borne in flat-topped clusters, and
are at first pink but finally pinkish white. This rose
is the parent of the Baltimore Belle;
its strong shoots, Dr. Gray says,
grow from ten to twenty feet
in one season.

The swamp
rose (*Rosa Caro-
lina*) is frequently
found beside the road
leading through boggy districts;
it always grows on more or less
damp ground, and spreads its
stems from two to eight feet
outward from the root. In
Nantucket it grows in dense
thickets beside the swampy
edges of the ponds, near the
south shore, together with the

Prairie Rose.

cat-tail flag (*Typha latifolia*). I have also sketched
it as it grew beside the road leading from the village
of Siasconset to Sankaty Head light. This species
has from five to nine (usually seven) smooth, dull-
green, finely toothed leaflets. The stems are provided with strong hooked thorns; the sepals (the

pointed green leaflets which enfold the pink buds)
are generally deciduous.*   The delicate pink flowers
are borne in small clusters ; they greatly vary in
strength of tint. *Rosa*
Carolina is distribu-
ted from Maine to
Florida, and
westward to
Minnesota
and Miss-
issippi.

Rosa Carolina.

The dwarf wild rose (*Rosa lucida*), sometimes
called shining rose, grows from one to five feet high,
has stout stems armed with numerous more or less

* Gray describes the sepals of this rose as spreading and deciduous in his Manual, but in his Field, Forest, and Garden
Botany, edited by Prof. L. H. Bailey, no notice is taken of the
fact. I have also been reminded by Mrs. M. L. Owen, one of the
leading botanists of New England, of the deciduous character of
the sepals. Very probably, however, this is a general rule, not
without an occasional exception, as in two or three cases I have
found the withered leaflets still attached to the seed receptacle,
but while the latter was yet ruddy-colored.

hooked thorns, and about seven small, thick, usually *shining* leaflets, dark green above and *coarsely toothed*. The flowers are pale pink and grow singly as well as in clusters; the sepals are bristly, more or less long and slender, and are frequently notched. The stipules (flaring sides of the leaf-stem where it joins the main stem) of this species are dilated or broad; those of *Rosa Caroli-na* are long and nar-row. *Rosa lucida* is distributed from Newfoundland south-westward to eastern Pennsylvania ; it blooms [earlier than *Rosa Carolina*] in June or July.

Rosa humilis is a species somewhat sim-ilar to the foregoing, but it extends as far West and Southwest as Minnesota and Lou-

Rosa lucida.

isiana. It is common, however, in drier soil or on rocky slopes. It grows from one to three feet high, and has slender, less leafy stems with nearly straight thorns.   The stipules are usually narrow, and, Gray says, in a few instances somewhat dilated.   The leaflets are also larger, thinner, and *dull* green.   The flowers are very often solitary and the sepals are nearly always lobed.

The early wild rose (*Rosa blanda*) is characterized by its thornless stems ; only occasionally it is found with a few and very rarely with numerous straight, weak thorns. It grows on stony banks and beside rocks, and its stem is from one to three feet high.   Its leaf is composed of from five to seven somewhat *wedge-shaped* and blunt leaflets, pale in color and a trifle hoary beneath ; the stipules are large and plain-edged, or rarely they are slightly toothed.   The light-pink flowers are large and bloom in late spring or early summer ; they are either solitary or grow two or three in a cluster ; the fruit is nearly globular.   *Rosa blanda* is distributed locally through New England, and is common in central

Rosa humilis.

New York, Orchard Lake and Munroe, Mich., La
Salle County, Ill., and the vicinity of the Great
Lakes.

Besides these five indigenous species which I have
described, there are two other *brier* roses which have

On the South Shore of Orchard Lake, Oakland Co., Michigan.

come to us from Europe, both of which are to be
found on many roadsides, especially near old farm-
houses. The first of these is the Eglantine or sweetbrier (*Rosa rubiginosa*), which came over from England with the early settlers. This rose may at once
be distinguished from all others by the aromatic
fragrance of its crushed leaves. The small, roundish,

double-toothed leaflets, five to seven on a stem, are lined beneath with russet-colored glands, which are accountable for the sweet scent. The small, pink flowers are mostly solitary, and the long, thorny branches are disposed to climb. The fruit is pear-shaped; that of *Rosa blanda* is nearly globular.

The second brier rose is the dog rose (*Rosa canina*), which is extremely common along the roadsides of New England; it is distributed quite generously through some parts of New Jersey, eastern Pennsylvania, and southern New York, and is even found as far Southwest as Tennessee. This species is very similar to the foregoing, but it lacks the aromatic fragrance. Sometimes the branches are unarmed, but frequently they are quite thorny; the flowers grow

Rosa blanda.

Seed vessels in two forms of Rosa blanda.

from two to four in a cluster or they are solitary.
The sepals are bordered with tiny leaflets, and they
are deciduous; the fruit is oblong ovate or
nearly globular. This rose has also
come to us from Europe.

Passing, now, the multi-
tudinous roses under cultivation and the interest
which is attached to
their pedigree, we come
to three beautiful spe-
cies, commonly seen
in parks and private
grounds, which I can not
leave without at least
a word of commenda-
tion. These are the
Burnet or Scotch rose
(*Rosa spinosissima*),
the Japanese rose (*Ro-
sa rugosa*), and the
trailing rose (*Rosa
Wichuraiana*). The Scotch rose grows about two
feet high and is exceedingly thorny; it bears most
charming, delicate yellow (sometimes white or pink),
early blooming flowers, which are a delight to the
eye in early summer. The leaves are composed of

Sweetbrier.

from seven to nine small, roundish leaflets.   The
Japanese rose is remarkable for its superb, dark-
green, bushy foliage; the single flowers are white or
pink and the large nearly globular fruit orange-red.
This rose blooms in early sum-
mer, but its great charm,
I think, is its luxuri-
ant, ornamental foli-
age.   The trailing
rose * (*Rosa Wi-
churaiana*) is ex-
tensively   planted
among   the   stony
borders   and   rocky
ledges of parks; it creeps
rapidly over the ground and sends
out in one season stems fully ten
feet long; it bears single white flowers; the tiny thick leaflets are shining

Dog Rose.

dark green.   This rose, which is also Japanese, is
one of the most charming of the *single* kind in cultivation; it is remarkably hardy.   It is quite common on the borders of the roads in the Arnold arboretum.   Very closely related to the roses are the
whitethorns or hawthorns.   Only three or four spe-

---

* Catalogued and sold under the name of Memorial Rose by
Peter Henderson & Co., seedsmen, New York.

cies are common in the North, the rest are Southern.

The scarlet-fruited thorn (*Cratægus coccinea*) appears frequently on the borders of the highway near the old farmhouse, and we may recognize it at once by its ornamentally notched and toothed leaf, and its dull-scarlet, tiny, apple-shaped fruit. The branches are beset with thorns about an inch long. Another species (*Cratægus Crus-galli*) bears thorns from *two to four* inches long, and also small apple-shaped fruit. The leaves are wedge-shaped, thick, and dark green. This species is frequently found in the thickets by the roadsides throughout the North. But one of the handsomest of the thorns is called *Cratægus mollis* (C. S. Sargent). This has large leaves, flowers, and fruit; it is commonly planted in parks. It blooms fully two weeks earlier than *C. coccinea*, and may readily be distinguished from that species by its densely woolly or hairy shoots. Its range is from eastern Massachusetts to Missouri and Texas. Chief among the thorns which are planted in our parks is the English hawthorn (*Cratægus oxyacantha*); but this is too well known to need description here. There are kinds with double pink or white flowers. Two other species are also found in the North and West, named *Cratægus tomentosa* and *Cratægus punctata*; the former is characterized by small ill-scented

6

flowers, large leaves which are densely woolly beneath, and obovate fruit, and the latter by small leaves and more or less white-dotted red or yellow fruit quite an inch in diameter. *Crataegus tomentosa* is distributed westward from eastern New York, but the other species is common throughout the North and extends as far South as Georgia.

The last member of the Rose subfamily is the shad bush, or Juneberry (*Amelanchier Canadensis*); sometimes it is called service berry. This shrub we are quite sure to see beside the road, particularly in dry wooded places. It has charmingly plain, shiny, evenly toothed leaves with a smooth texture; the flowers, which appear just before the leaves, hang in large, drooping, white clusters; the petals are long and narrow. The fruit, ripe in June, resembles the huckleberry, and in different stages of development is buff, flesh-color, pink, red, purple, and black-purple; indeed, it is even more beautiful than the graceful flowers, and is edible besides; up in the back country it is called "sugar plums." The shad bush is distributed throughout the North and South; westward its limit is on a line reaching from Minnesota to Louisiana. Throughout the southern region of the White Mountains, and in the vicinity of Mount Monadnoc it is common on the borders of meadow and road.

The third subfamily (Pear) includes the pear, apple, and quince trees, and the chokeberry and mountain ash.

The chokeberry (*Pyrus arbutifolia*), is indeed as unacceptable to the palate as the name seems to imply ; but I have noticed that the birds do not consider the puckery taste of the berry so objectionable, as they often appear to enjoy the fruit in the late fall when there are many other berries still clinging to the bushes.

Damp ground is the chosen place of the chokeberry, and it is generally found in the thickets beside the bridge, not far from where the

The Chokeberry.

Phœbe bird loves to build her nest. It grows from one to three feet high, has somewhat narrow, toothed, sharply pointed leaves, and white or pinkish flowers, which grow in flattish clusters at the ends of the branches. The fruit is dull purple, small, pear-shaped, or nearly round, and *very astringent*; it clings to the branch after the leaves have fallen.

The chokeberry is common from New England to Florida ; westward its limitation is Minnesota, Illinois, Missouri, and Louisiana. *Pyrus nigra* (Sargent) is a species with broader, reverse, egg-shaped leaves, earlier flowers, and larger black fruit, which soon falls.

Nearly related to the chokeberry is the beautiful mountain ash (*Pyrus Americana*), which, however, is more of a tree than a shrub. Its pretty sumach-like compound leaves, and its bright scarlet berries, about as large as peas, are very often seen beside the highways which lead through the Northern States, and it may easily be identified by its aromatic wild-cherry odor when bruised. Another species with broader and somewhat blunt leaves, called *Pyrus sambucifolia*, is common among the mountains of northern New Hampshire and Vermont ; it is not likely to be seen beside the road, however, unless planted there.

The last member of the Rose Family to which I will draw attention is the Japan quince (*Pyrus Japonica*, or *Cydonia Japonica*). This is a familiar roadside character of parks and gardens. In the Arnold arboretum, near Boston, there are several varieties of the beautiful shrub, which, it seems to me, should be more commonly cultivated. These are *P.*

Japonica atrosanguinea, deep-scarlet blossoms; *P. Japonica rosea*, scarlet-pink blossoms; *P. Japonica Moorlosi*, variegated rose-red and nearly white blossoms; and *P. Japonica Mallardi*, scarlet blossoms.

Nevertheless, the *Pyrus Japonica* is an old favorite which will hardly lose its popularity, for in April (in the North in the middle of May) this shrub puts forth its leaves and beautiful scarlet apple-blossom-shaped flowers long before anything else shows a sign of responding to the spring weather. It will be found among the shrubbery of Prospect Park, Brooklyn, and Central Park, New York.

The thoroughly Japanesque character of *Pyrus Japonica* is revealed in its spring colors when the leaves are just unfolding. In almost any position on the garden grounds it is suggestive of the artistic kakemono. A more beautiful picture than that which it forms against the soft-gray background of an old weatherbeaten board fence is unimaginable. The ruddy tinge of the budding foliage, the brilliant scarlet of the blossoms in broad sunshine, the rugged tracery of the slender brown twigs with perhaps the azure blue of some dainty bluebird visitor (the bluebird is very frequently attracted by the red flowers)—all these uncommon colors and picturesque lines are peculiarly like the vigorous decorations which we may see on some Japanese screen. Yet I have no doubt but what the *Pyrus Japonica* is scarcely thought to be more than a familiar scarlet-flowered shrub of ordinary interest; and it seems as though it was most frequently planted for a hedge with a careless indifference about environment.

CHAPTER V.

SOME of the most beautiful shrubs and herbs which grow beside the woodland road are members of the Heath family (*Ericaceæ*), and many of them—

the huckleberry, trailing arbutus, mountain laurel, and Indian pipe, for instance — are common throughout the hilly regions of Pennsylvania, New Jersey, New York, and New England.

As summer advances we will find on the way-sides of the climbing hills

Dwarf Blueberry.

the dwarf blueberry (*Vaccinium Pennsylvanicum*), with its beautiful cadet-blue berries, sweet as honey, clustered at the tips of bushes scarcely ten inches high. The miniature leaves are variously colored

71

with red and green, finely toothed and laurel-shaped. It is the lowest and earliest of the blueberries. Its immature clusters of fruit are of the most beautiful æsthetic hues: green, magenta, pink, purple, and violet. The dwarf blue-berry is an upland species which is found on some of the highest summits of the White Mountains. Another species, *V. Canadense*, has downy leaves without teeth, which are broader than those of *V. Pennsylvanicum*; it grows from one to two feet high. Late in August, in the thickets that border the marsh, the fruit of the swamp or high blueberry (*V. corymbosum*) appears. This lowland species attains a height of from five to ten feet, and bears a blue-purple or blackish, slightly acid berry. In May the flowering branchlets are often leafless.

Huckleberry.

The common huckleberry (*Gaylussacia resinosa*) grows from one to three feet high, and bears a shining *black* berry without bloom, which ripens in August. Its leaf (without teeth) and reddish flower in May or early June are sticky with bright, tiny, resinous yellowish globules. We will find this species growing on the rocky hillside, or on the border of the wooded swamp. It does not occur in the White Mountains, where the dwarf blueberry is very common, but it is plentiful in various parts of New Jersey, on the island of Nantucket, Lake George, N. Y., and in Putnam County, N. Y.; it is widely distributed from Maine to northern Georgia.

The squaw huckleberry (*V. stamineum*), sometimes called deerberry, is a rugged shrub two to three feet high, very much branched, bearing large, greenish or yellowish, globular or pear - shaped, hanging berries, which are insipid and not edible; they ripen in September.

Squaw Huckleberry.

The flowers of all these shrubs are vase-shaped and five-cleft at the edge, usually of a whitish, pinkish, or magentaish hue, and they appear in spring or early summer. The common cranberry of our markets (*Vaccinium macrocarpon*) is found in the peat bogs of the Northern States, and flowers in June.

The beautiful miniature, creeping snowberry (*Chiogenes serpyllifolia*) belongs in the peat bogs and mossy woods of the North, but it very frequently finds its way to the borders of the mountain road; we can always tell it by the flavor of wintergreen in both leaf and berry. The leaves are tiny and ovate-pointed, the minute flowers grow solitary at the junction of the leaf with the main stem, and bloom in May, and the clear, snow-white berries appear in late summer. It is certainly the daintiest member of the Heath family. I very frequently find it in the damp woods of the White Mountains.

On the rocky hillsides of New Jersey and Pennsylvania, and distributed in the far North and the West as far as Missouri, is the low-growing little plant called bearberry (*Arctostaphylos Uva-Ursi*). Its small leaves are thick and evergreen, and it trails over the barren, stony ground, much as the arbutus does, but in thick mats. The leaves are toothless and smooth. The flowers appear in May; they are urn-shaped, flesh-color pink-tipped, and are succeeded by astringent red berries, which are mealy and flavorless; as they remain on the plants through the winter, they furnish acceptable food for the winter birds. The species *A. alpina*, with de-

Creeping Snowberry.

MOUNT POCOMOONSHINE,
ADIRONDACKS.
ESSEX CO., N. Y.

THE BEARBERRY.

ciduous, toothed, strongly veined leaves and black fruit, is common on the high summits of the White Mountains.

The bearberry may also be found on many of the stony slopes of the Adirondack Mountains. I have sketched that most interesting eastern rocky outpost of these northern hills called Mount Pocomoonshine, on whose precipitous cliffs the bearberry finds here and there a scant foothold. The grand old mountain faces the road about eight miles south of Keeseville.

The common wintergreen or cheekerberry (*Gaultheria procumbens*), with its pure red berry and dark, varnished, evergreen leaf, is too well known to need description here. It is very frequently found on the wooded roadsides.

The beautiful staggerbush (*Andromeda Mariana*)* has ample clusters of nodding flowerets, urn-shaped, white, and waxy, which appear in spring or early summer on nearly leafless branchlets.

Bearberry in flower.

---

* It is said to be poisonous to cattle.

This is a familiar shrub of the roadside in low grounds, which is becoming common in cultivation; it grows from two to four feet high. Very closely related to the Andromeda is the sorrel tree or sour-wood (*Oxydendrum arboreum*), whose leaves are about the size and shape of those of the peach. The dainty little white, urn-shaped flowers appear in June or July; they are borne in long one-sided clusters, and strongly resemble those of the Andromeda. I have never seen the sorrel tree growing wild in New England; it is found quite commonly in the rich woods of Pennsylvania, and is distributed westward as far as Indiana and central Tennessee. There is a good specimen under cultivation at the Arnold arboretum, near Boston.

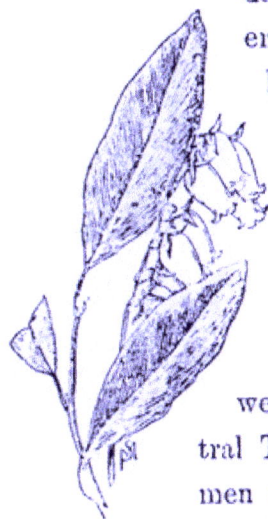

Andromeda.

A most charming shrub which is frequently seen on the roadsides of the coast States, North and South, particularly in the pine barrens of New Jersey, is *Leucothœ racemosa*; this has beautiful long, upright but slightly curved racemes of flowers, white, fragrant, and drooping. Each spike is from three to four inches long, with from twelve to eighteen (sometimes more) urn-shaped blossoms. The leaves are from one to two inches long, smooth, pointed, and sharply toothed. This shrub grows from four to ten feet high, and blooms in May or June, but the scaly bracted flower spikes are formed during the preceding summer. It is certainly deserving of wide cultivation.

Still another similar shrub which blooms in May, the leather leaf (*Cassandra calyculata*), formerly confused with the species Andromeda, is commonly found beside the road which passes over low, wet grounds near the coast; it is frequently seen in the pine barrens of New Jersey in company with *Leucothœ*. The tiny, white, urn-shaped flowers are evenly distributed over the branchlets, each one growing in the axil of the small leaf. About twenty of these smaller leaves occupy a six-inch terminal length of the branchlets, forming with the pretty flowers a one-sided decorative cluster. The leather leaf is well named, for its leaves are thick and leathery, shiny above and rust-colored beneath, about an inch long, tough, nearly if not quite free from teeth, and almost evergreen. It grows from two to three feet high

Leather Leaf.

and is thickly branched. Its geographical distribution is from Maine to Minnesota, and southward to Georgia.

Closely related to the shrubs already mentioned, and more beautiful in the larger development of its decorative, frosty, waxy, white flowers is the familiar mountain laurel (*Kalmia latifolia*). This shrub reaches its finest growth in Pennsylvania and New Jersey, where it forms, on damp ground, dense thickets from four to ten and sometimes thirty feet high. In May or June it is in full blossom, and its showy clusters of pink-tinged buds and flowers I regard as the most beautiful of all our early wild flowers. The flowers of the kalmia must be seen under a magnifying glass to be thoroughly appreciated, and it is scarcely necessary for me to add that this revelation of its perfect form and beauty will create a lasting impression on one's memory. No other wild flower possesses such exact symmetry, and few, if any such splendid frosty sheen. Kalmia is distributed chiefly along the mountains, from Maine to western Florida. Its lance-ovate leaves differ from the preceding species in being much larger, as well as bright green and smooth on both sides.

The crowning glory of the Heath family is the rhododendron. The flower which we see in the public parks in early June is most likely to be a hybrid

THE BATTLE GROUND AND BRIDGE. CONCORD, MASS.

of *Rhododendron Catawbiense* (a native species) and
R. arboreum; the latter is a species which comes
from the Himalayas, and is not hardy. *R. Ponticum*
is a species from Asia Minor, hardy in the North, but
only as a low shrub; this has a dark magenta-purple
flower, which appears in late spring. The hybrid
rhododendrons are of various colors; those partaking
chiefly of the *Catawbiense* characteristics are distinguished by broad, flat, broad-pointed glossy leaves, and
purple or light lilac-blue flowers. A prominent characteristic of the rhododendron is the large conical
bud which passes through the severe cold of our
Northern winters unharmed, and the gracefully
drooping, evergreen leaves clustered in a circle below
the bud which terminates the branchlet.

Beside the road where the swampy ground meets
its borders we will possibly meet in May the "leafless
blooms" of the delicate magenta-pink rhodora (*Rhododendron Rhodora*), about the charms of which
Emerson sang. I never thought the flower a "rival
of the rose," nor have I been particularly impressed
with its beauty; its color is too near the unpopular
magenta to make it a favorite with anybody but an
enthusiastic poet. But the magenta flower is extremely dainty in form, and so long as the tardy New
England spring brings a mere handful of rival blossoms, this one appears as beautiful and showy as one

could wish. The flowers appear before the somewhat hairy, pale-green leaves. The shrub grows from
one to three feet high, with each stem divided into
four or five branchlets, which are terminated by the
encircling flower clusters. The rhodora is readily
found in the vicinity of Concord and Lexington,
Mass. It is also seen in cultivation in the Arnold
arboretum near Boston, and the Harvard Botanic
Garden, Cambridge.

The great laurel (*Rhododendron maxima*) is
somewhat rare from Maine to Ohio, but quite common in the mountains of Pennsylvania and southward. It has large, thick leaves, and showy pink or
white flowers, which bloom in July or August. It is
a tall shrub, from six to twenty feet high, frequently
found on the wooded banks of mountain streams.
We are not likely to meet it on the roadside, but a
near relation is far more apt to adorn the wooded
borders of the highway, at least in the southern part
of New York; this is the purple azalea or pinxter
flower (*Rhododendron nudiflorum*), which grows
from three to six feet high, and bears handsome
blossoms an inch and a half across, slightly fragrant,
and variously colored with pink, magenta, and pale
yellow. This shrub is usually found on the banks of
sluggish streams and the borders of swamps; it is
not very common on the wooded roadsides in New

England, and is only occasionally found on those of the Middle States. In the South it is quite abundant.

The swamp honeysuckle (*Rhododendron viscosum*) is a somewhat sticky white - flowered azalea, which grows on the borders of swamps, quite commonly in the southern parts of New England. It blooms in June, and is usually found not far from the roadside in the marshes near the coast.

Rhododendron viscosum.

Quite an amount of the swamp honeysuckle may be gathered early in the summer in the swampy borders of the roads near Buzzard's Bay and Wood's Holl, Mass. While we are still on the highway which passes through the cold, damp, wooded glens of the Northern hills we may look for the shrub known as Labrador tea (*Ledum latifolium*); it grows in cold bogs or

Labrador Tea.

7

woods from New England to Pennsylvania, Michigan, Minnesota, and northward. The leaves are about two inches long, very white-woolly or velvety beneath, narrow, like willow leaves, and without teeth, but strongly rolled at the edge. The flowers are small, white, and the little corollas have five distinct petals. They appear in May and June and sometimes continue through July. The shrub grows from one to five feet high. In olden times its astringent leaves were used as a substitute for tea.

One of the most attractive and fragrant members of the Heath family is the white alder or sweet pepper bush (*Clethra alnifolia*). This beautiful shrub is as worthy of cultivation as the shad bush or the mountain laurel. Not infrequently it appears in the water borders of our parks. The leaves are from two to four inches long, wedge-shaped, and toothed at the upper edge. The small flowers appear in July or August, in long, terminal, upright spikes. They are similar in form to those of Labrador tea, but they have in addition a sweet, heavy

Clethra.

odor. This shrub is common in the dense copses
that flank the marshes near the coast, from Maine to
Georgia. The perfume of the white alder, like that
of the common milkweed, is cloyingly sweet, but both
odors, as I remember them, are pleasantly reminis-
cent of the heat and drowsy idleness of midsummer,
and they are inseparable from the peaceful hum of
the bumblebee, the intermittent *"zipping"* of the
green grasshopper (*Orchelimum vulgare*), and the
vigorous, loud *s-szip, s-szip, s-szip* of the greener,
cone-headed grasshopper (*Conocephalus ensiger*).
Clethra grows from three to ten feet high, and is so
beautiful when in full bloom that I greatly wonder
why it is not in common cultivation; but, like *Cassandra, Andromeda, Leucothœ,* and several other
splendid members of the Heath family, it is left to
bloom in its native wilds, while innumerable foreign
species of less attractive appearance are put in the
gardener's hands for him to nurse with arduous care,
resulting in indifferent success through our rigorous
Northern winters.

There are four other lesser members of this interesting family, all of which are common on the
wooded road. The first of these is prince's pine or
pipsissewa (*Chimaphila umbellata*). This beautiful
little evergreen-leaved plant puts forth its waxy,
flesh-pink blossoms in June and July. Let us look

at a single flower under the magnifying glass.   What a revelation of dainty, frosty beauty it is!   There are five petals which are cream-white or pale flesh-colored; these are well turned back in the mature flower, and just inside of them we see a narrow circle of subdued magenta, over which are displayed in high relief ten handsome brown-purple anthers which are conspicuously two-horned.   In the center of all rises a tiny, pink-yellow tinged dome.   Not only is the little flower beautiful, but it is filled with a rare and delicate perfume.   We may look for it beneath the spruce and pine trees on dry needle-covered ground.   Not far from the pipsissewa we may also see the shin leaf (*Pyrola elliptica*), whose nodding flowers with prominent, curved, taillike styles are also waxy, but greenish white.   The dull - green, somewhat spoon-shaped leaves rise in a circle from the base of the plant.   The flower stem is from six to nine inches high.

Pipsissewa.

I have found the pipsissewa and the shin leaf growing side by side in the woods about Saddle River Valley, N. J., and on the borders of the woodland roads which skirt the mountains of New

Hampshire; but both flowers are common throughout the Northern States.

The last two members of the Heath family are the daintiest and oddest of all; these are the ghostly white Indian pipe (*Monotropa uniflora*), with its frail, fleshy single flower familiar to us all, and the tawny or reddish false beech drops (*Monotropa Hypopitys*). We find the latter on the borders of oak or pine woods, flowering in summer time. The stem is from four to ten inches high, and bears tiny fragrant flowers with four or five petals of a ruddy, or pale terra-cotta hue.

The *Monotropas* are common throughout the East. They flourish on the decomposed vegetation of damp rich woods.

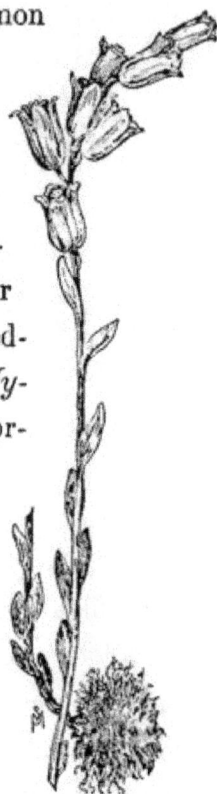

False Beech
Drops.

CHAPTER VI

THE soft bleating note that comes to our ears from the marsh in summer time is that of the so-called tree toad (*Hyla versicolor*), who was given his Latin name because he possesses an extraordinary ability to assume a color analogous with his surroundings. (*Metachrosis* is the term usually employed, meaning a shifting over from one color to another.)   But it is a slow process with the little animal, who really requires quite a little time to "get over" from dull brown to bright green.   He does this, however, and, according to the brown trunk, green leaf, gray stone, or green-white lichen on which he is perched, proceeds to

Tree Toad.

match colors as a lady would in the purchasing of dress material. He is most commonly arrayed in warm gray.

The figure of the tree toad is not as charming as its voice or its color. He is covered with large and small warty excrescences from top to toe, and there is a prominent loose fold of skin across his yellow-white breast. He is short and stumpy in head and limb, as well as broad-toed ; in fact, he is not aristocratic looking like his cousins *Acris* and *Pickeringii*. But his voice possesses a most winning, pathetic quality which I can only liken to the musical, bubbling bleat of a miniature lamb; there is something attractive and soothing about it. This should not be confused with the song of the common toad (*Bufo Americanus*), which can be closely imitated by whistling the note C two octaves above middle C and humming, *sotto voce*, A in the second octave below middle C, thus :

The tone is sustained uniformly for about four seconds, then an answer comes from across the pond a musical third lower—A in the treble and E in the bass.

Later in the summer we hear the combined voices of these singers in the hedges, by the roadside fence, in the orchard, and even on the border of the wood. In the northern parts of Vermont and New Hampshire I have rarely heard *Hyla versicolor*; but in the Highlands of the Hudson, on Long Island, and in various localities of New Jersey his voice is a very familiar one to me. The tone is not prolonged beyond two seconds (rarely a trifle over this), and it is characterized by a well-marked crepitation. The drowsy, droning voice of the common toad as he sings in the marshes in early summer is dual-toned and far more musical; indeed, it has all the mysterious charm of a soothing lullaby, and in my own mind it is intimately associated with the romantic, slow, introductory movement of Beethoven's so-called Moonlight Sonata, a fitting musical interpretation of the peace and quiet of summer life in the country, just as the last, impetuous, hurried movement is interpretative of the restless, wearing life of the city.

Among the singers of the meadow not one is quite as attractive in appearance as the beautiful, pale, ivory-colored tree cricket (*Œcanthus niveus*). He is sometimes called the "snowy tree cricket," as his ethereal body and glassy wings suggest a color which is the very antithesis of black. The song of this little creature does not issue from the grass, but from some tall weed stem or tree trunk. The tone

THE HIGHLANDS OF THE
HUDSON, AT WEST POINT,
ORANGE CO., N. Y.

THE TREE CRICKET,
ŒCANTHUS NIVEUS.

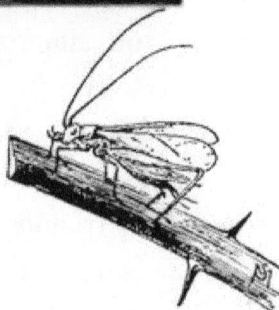

is usually pitched in E and it recurs with rhythmical
precision.   Burroughs calls the *Œcanthus* the " purr-

ing cricket," and speaks of its song as coming " in
waves," which is not only true of the soloist but of
the general chorus.   The sound is regularly tossed
back and forth like those sustained chords which
occur early in the first movement of Beethoven's
Fifth Symphony, but the musical effect of the grand
chorus is a distinct alternation of two tones thus :

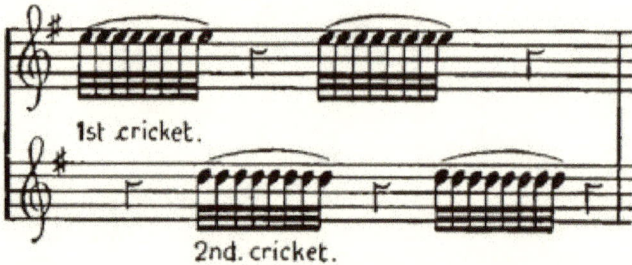

an exact counterpart of the opening notes of the
scherzo in the Third Symphony.   How under the

moonlight (not sun!) it was possible for the great Beethoven to so exactly reproduce the music which one hears at night in midsummer among the Highlands of the Hudson in the vicinity of Anthony's Nose and Storm King without ever having set his foot upon American soil it is difficult to imagine! For there are no singing fields in the old country, comparatively speaking; the meadows of England, Tuscany, or Switzerland in May, June, or August are silent—that, at least, is my remembrance of them. And I may also add that a field in the White Mountain region of New Hampshire is only half musical, again comparatively speaking. The meadow music which one may hear at twilight on Long Island, Staten Island, in the Catskill Mountains, in the Highlands of the Hudson, around Lake Mahopac in Putnam County, and in the vicinity of Niagara Falls, N. Y., in Saddle River, Bergen County, and the counties of Monmouth, Atlantic, and Salem in New Jersey, and in various parts of Delaware, Maryland, and Virginia, is *far* beyond what one will hear in either Maine or New Hampshire. I refer exclusively to insect music. On or about the first of September, when the wooded slopes of the Navesink Highlands, New Jersey, are thrilling with the songs of crickets and katydids, the woods and fields of northern New Hampshire are almost silent. But we can not expect

EAGLE CLIFF, FRANCONIA NOTCH,
WHITE MOUNTAINS, N. H.

everything all at once or in just one place; so it is
the case that the woods of New Jersey do not know
the song of the hermit thrush, but the forest glens beneath Eagle Cliff and Mount Kinsman, in the Franconia Range, N. H., echo his music from June until
August.

But I must return to our tree crickets. The little
Œcanthus niveus begins his trilling song at sunset
and continues it throughout the night. He tunes his
fiddle about the end of July, and does not finish his
concert until the autumn days grow cold. I understand that the female of this species deposits her eggs
in the pithy stems of the raspberry and blackberry
vines and thereby causes much trouble for the small-
fruit grower.

Another closely allied species is called the broad-
winged climbing cricket (*Œcanthus
latipennis*). This cricket is
larger than the preceding, and
differs very slightly in
color from it; it is
ivory - white. The
elytra—that is, the two
superior wing covers—
are glassy and perfectly

Broad-winged Climbing Cricket.

transparent. It differs from the species *Œ. niveus*
in having the top of the head and lower half of the

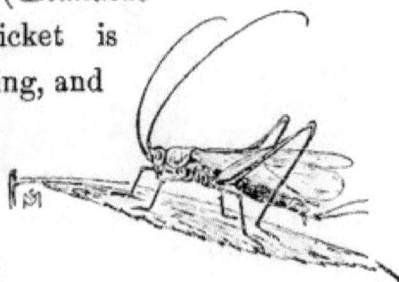

antennæ suffused with *pink or pink-brown* ; it also generally, if not always, lacks the small gray-brown spots which are invariably present in *Œ. niveus* on the lower face of the two lowest joints of the antennæ. The song of this broad-winged cricket need not be confused with that of *Œ. niveus* ; it is like a continuous, shrill, high-pitched rattle-whistle.

Œcanthus latipennis, it is said, prefers the shoots of the grapevine in which to lay its eggs. It is distributed southward and westward, but doubtfully as far Northwest as Rock Island, Ill. It does not occur in the Northeastern States.

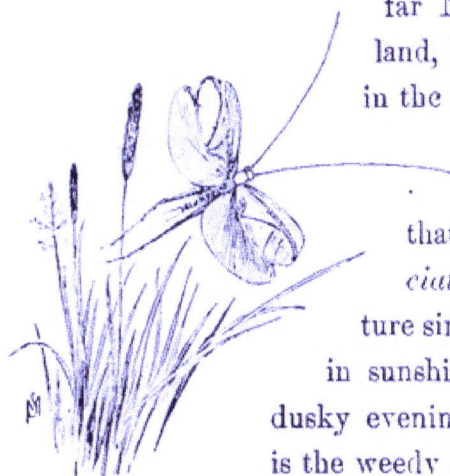

The most remarkable tree cricket is that named *Œcanthus fasciatus*. This little creature sings all day and all night, in sunshine, cloud shadow, and dusky evening. Its favorite resort is the weedy roadside, or the hedges where tall sunflowers and goldenrods abound. It sings about the

Tree Cricket
(*Œ. fasciatus*).

middle of August and continues until the time of frost. The predominating color of the wings is white tinted green, but the body varies from an ivory-white marked with gray-brown to black. In typical speci-

mens the head and its vicinity are whitish, with three
distinct gray-brown or dark-brown stripes. The song
of *Œ. fasciatus* is shrill and rapid; it is varied in
length, lasting from two or three seconds to one or
two minutes without interruption. During the performance the wings of tree crickets are raised to a
perpendicular position and vibrate so rapidly that the
motion is not discernible. The notes of *Œ. fasciatus*
occur at the rate of from twelve to sixteen a second,
thus :

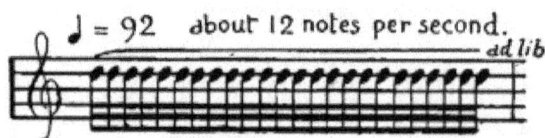

These marvelous little musicians with the glassy
wings can outdo the swiftest " presto " of the piano
virtuoso, by producing nearly *one thousand* notes per
minute! The geographical range of *Œ. fasciatus* is
the same as that of *Œ. niveus*, from southern New
England to Indiana, Illinois, Iowa, and southward.*
It is larger than *Œ. niveus* and has the longest antennæ of all the species.

Œcanthus angustipennis is a narrow-winged species, less common in the West than the species
already mentioned, and more at home in the broad

---

* Œ. fasciatus is reported as abundant along the roadsides of
Champaign Co., Illinois.

meadows than *Œ. fasciatus*.   The species *Œ. angus-tipennis*, *Œ. latipennis*, and *Œ. niveus* prefer the cultivated field to the weedy wayside.

This slender cricket is white, deeply suffused with green, has longer and slenderer hind legs than those of the other species, and a smaller head.   The song resembles that of *Œ. fasciatus*, but is less shrill, and lasts but from three to five seconds, with inter-vals of corresponding length.

The song is usually heard at night.   Both the song and the singer have been confusedly

Narrow-winged Tree
Cricket.

connected with the rhythmical *Œ. niveus*; an atten-tive ear, however, can not fail to detect a wide differ-ence in the songs.   *Œ. niveus* utters its *t-re-ee, t-re-ee, t-re-ee*, in metronome time, fifty trills occurring in a minute—Jerome McNeil says seventy, but I give the results of my own personal experience.   In different kinds of weather crickets sing faster or slower.   In the case of *Œ. angustipennis* the song is slower than that of *Œ. niveus*.

The tree crickets are remarkable for their rhyth-

mical music, and however out of time the voices
may be for a short season, they inevitably become synchronous or antiphonal, and to my ear
some large section of the grand chorus is *always* antiphonal. This perfectly charming effect of musical
tones being tossed back and fourth, which I have
already referred to as exactly reproducing the opening notes of the scherzo in Beethoven's Fifth Symphony, is what Thoreau heard when he likened the
sound to "slumberous breathing," and what William
Hamilton Gibson called "a pulsating vesper chorus
. . . a lullaby between the evening and the morning
twilights." Hawthorn describes it as an "audible
stillness," and makes his Canterbury poet think "that
if moonlight could be heard, it would sound just like
that." Of all the music in the moonlit field which
holds our ears entranced as we linger on the highway, this is the sweetest and best; it is the cricket's
love song! I often wonder why Irving did not
allude to it in the Legend of Sleepy Hollow, because just near the bridge where the superstitious
schoolmaster "lost his head" the music of *Œ. niveus*
is rife from late August to the time when the days
grow cold.*

---

* As the night when the schoolmaster rode abroad was a cloudy
one, possibly the tree crickets were not singing as usual; a warm
moonlight night is the best one for cricket music.

A far less musical singer than the tree cricket lives in the meadow grasses, and favors us in broadest daylight in the warm days of July with his *gip, gip, gip, gip-zee-e-e-e-e-e*! This is the common meadow grasshopper *Orchelimum vulgare.* He is *green*, and he has *long* antennæ, so he must not be confused with the short, stumpy-feelered, red-legged locust, who is wrongly called a grasshopper. The *Orchelimum* is a delicately modeled creature, about an inch long, with transparent wings through which one may readily see the green body. His legs are slender, and at the shoulder end of each wing is the hard, glassy formation which, when the wing is rapidly vibrated, rubs on the concave expansion of the other wing and causes the sharp, *zigging* sound. The locust

Meadow Grasshopper.

(grasshopper) in flying, in a very different way, produces a clapping or snapping sound with his wings.*

---

* See *Trimerotropis verruculata*, page 103.

The green grasshopper is a day singer, who revels in the noontime heat with the mercury standing at 90°.

The brown cricket (*Gryllus abbreviatus*),* common in the Middle States, who lives in the pastures and the grassy borders of the road, is a daylight and twilight singer; his sharp musical note also thrills interruptedly from sunset to sunrise along with the softer and more regular note of the white cricket. In June and July the meadows and wooded pastures are filled with the cricket's music. His chirp is fitful and shrill; it is not really a trill, but the rapid repetition of a single note from three to five times with irregular intervals. I can not rely on the black cricket for three-four time or six-eight time; he "gangs his ain gait," as the Scotchman would say, and leaves me and my metronome to go mine.

Brown Cricket, and tiny Spotted Cricket.

---

* *G. neglectus* is the most common New England cricket. *G. luctuosus* is also common; its fore wings are very long and project beyond the abdomen. It is one of our largest crickets.

This is not the case with the white cricket; he
is the soul of rhythmical accuracy. Our brown
cricket, like the grasshopper, makes his music by a
rapid vibration of his wings. The song is produced
by a rubbing together of the superior wings, which
are hard, glassy, and roughened on their contiguous
edges; thus, the rapid flitting of the wings produces
the musical stridulation—more musical and less strid-
ulous, however, than the grasshopper's zigging note.
It is, of course, scarcely necessary for me to remark
that it is not the female but the male insect who
is *always* the musician.

There are several species of crickets which are
common. The one I have already mentioned is most
generally found in fields and on roadsides; it is what
is called a social cricket—that is, it lives with its fellows and does not inhabit a burrow. Another common cricket (*Gryllus Pennsylvanicus*) burrows under
every stone in my garden; he is not a social character.

The tiny spotted cricket (*Nemobius vittatus*), of a
brownish striped color, is still another singer whose
spasmodic, interrupted chirp is constantly heard in
the fields during late summer and early autumn,
from New Hampshire to Maryland and Nebraska.
This musician has a variable song made up of a trill
and a sharp preparatory click, thus:

During his singing his wings are elevated at a considerable angle from the body.

Still another meadow singer is the cone-headed grasshopper (*Conocephalus ensiger*). This is the commonest species east of the Rocky Mountains, and the most familiar bright, light-green insect of the cultivated field, as well as the salt marshes near the seashore. Rarely he is a brownish straw color, but in any case his narrow, pointed forehead is a sufficient proof of his

Cone-headed Grasshopper.

identity; he is, besides, a very long, slender grasshopper, with extremely long fine feelers and a sharp, rasping voice, quite unlike that of any of the other meadow musicians. His note is an emphatic, suddenly loud *s-szip*, *s-szip*, *s-szip*, *s-szip*, continuous, rapid, and penetrating beyond description. In fact, it is one of the least interesting and most ear-ringing voices of the meadow or roadside. He is sharptoothed, too, as well as sharp-tongued, a fact which I have more than once ascertained by a too intimate acquaintance with the really handsome insect; but William Hamilton Gibson makes game of him, and calls him "the clown of all this heyday" so justly that we certainly should read Singing Wings * for the sake of this amusing and fuller description.

But speaking of " biters " reminds me of another sharp-toothed character, whose vicious nip is sometimes sufficiently tenacious to cause him the loss of his head. The katydid (*Microcentrum retinervis*) is a frequent singer on the highway in the evening hours. He looks like a large green grasshopper, but he has larger wings, which are leaflike and delicately veined; his antennæ are much longer than his body, and his slender, long legs give him a peculiarly distinguished appearance, quite superior to that of a plebeian grasshopper. The katydid lives among the trees and hides under the leaves in the daytime, but as soon as the sun sets emerges from seclusion and begins his "petulant and shrill" tirade. Dr. Holmes calls him a " testy little dogmatist," and, as William Hamilton Gibson remarks, falls into an excusable

---

* See Harper's Magazine for 1886, vol. lxxiii.

THE HIGHLANDS OF
NAVESINK,
MONMOUTH CO., N. J.

KATYDIDS,
CYRTOPHYLLUS CONCAVUS
  (ABOVE)
MICROCENTRUM RETINERVIS
  (BELOW).

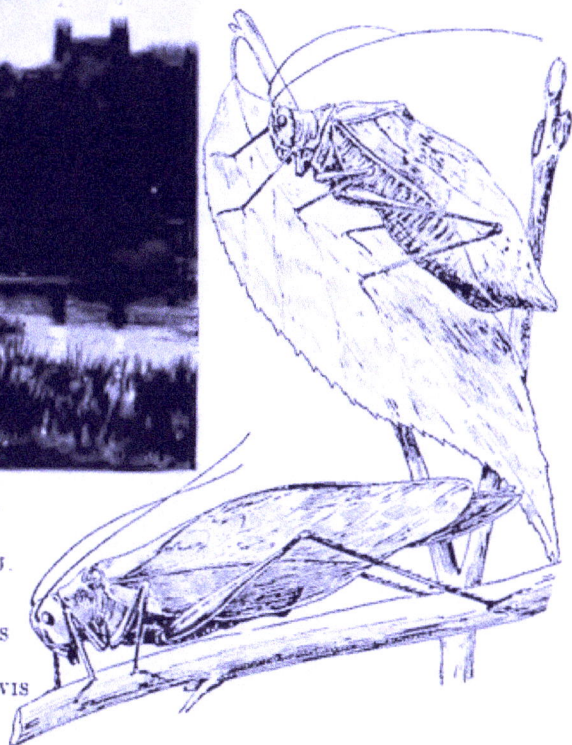

entomological error by accusing the particular insect which he heard of being a *female* with a quivering, trilling voice! But in this case, the truth is, the male insects do all the disputing. The katydid's voice is too familiar to need comment or description here. The tones are harsh and uttered in triplets like detached bits of the cicada's *zee-e-e-e-e* (the locust), but the method by which the noise is produced is curious. In the upper portion of each green wing cover, near the point where it is joined to the body, just where it overlaps the other, is a glassy formation set in a sort of frame; as the insect opens and shuts its wing covers, these frames strike each other, and the result is the *zig-zig-zig* which we know so well. On or about the first of September the wooded slopes of the Highlands of Navesink resound with the quarrelsome voices of these curious insects; in the White Mountains I do not recollect of having heard even a single disputer "having it all his own way."

There are two common species of the katydid, the one above described being the most abundant in the Northern States; it is usually called the angular-winged katydid. The other species, also common in the Central and Eastern States, is named *Cyrtophyllus concavus*; its wing covers are longer than its wings, and they are broadly convex.

The so-called grasshopper with very short feelers, who is usually decked out in a variety of colors, is really a locust. The commonest species in our Eastern fields is called *Melanoplus femur-rubrum*, or, in straight English, the red-legged locust.* This destructive insect is widely distributed over the United States east of the Rocky Mountains. It swarms on the

Red-legged Locust.

grassy intervales of the White Mountain region, and covers the broad meadows of New Jersey; it is everywhere, and always a perfect nuisance, devouring every green thing, and even relishing the flavor of a silk umbrella or a dainty muslin dress.†

Beware the locust! for besides his awkward habit

Melanoplus atlanis, similar to M. femur-rubrum.

of staining one's clothing with "molasses," he will make a dainty repast off a silk handkerchief or the printed flowers of a lawn dress! His song is a somewhat *pianissimo z-ee-e-e-e*, which is produced by

---

* Another common species is *Melanoplus atlanis*, similar to the one described.

† In Canada and New England some years ago his ravages were particularly extensive and destructive.

scraping or rubbing his legs against his hard-shell wing covers; he is, in fact, a veritable fiddler in the grand orchestra of the meadow. One musician does not count for much in the noontime symphony of the singing wings, but when two hundred thousand bowstrings are in full swing there can be no doubt about who supplies the orchestra with its first violins! Although the locust's music is but an obligato accompaniment to the high-pitched, ringing voices of the soloists, it soothes the ear with a drowsy hum, which is the very embodiment of midsummer peace and "audible stillness."

A rather large locust (*Trimerotropis verruculata*) is quite common on the intervales of the White Mountain district. This creature flies like a bird, and snaps his wings at will during his devious flight. He skims along with a sudden *klack, klack, klack, klack,*

X, Left wing of Œ. niveus, showing the portion from A to B used for singing. Z, Left wing of Orchelimum, showing the vein in black at C used for singing. Both drawings are copied from cuts found in several publications —neither are true to nature; compare with the succeeding drawing of niveus wing, and the wing on drawing of Orchelimum.

and gives a dip at each "klack," much in the same fashion that the yellowbird utters its joyous chirrup during its undulating flight through the twilight sky.

This insect is most commonly seen in the latter part of August and throughout September; it is very common on the meadows of Campton, N. H.

The locust called *Stenobothrus curtipennis*, a very common species at once recognized by its very short wings, also sings in the Campton meadows. This musician uses both legs at once, and scrapes his wing covers in somewhat syncopated time. But to distinguish his music from that of the other members of the orchestra is a difficult task. His hissing notes, given out at the rate of six to a second, continue for about two seconds, then a short pause and *da capo*. This music is not nearly as loud as that of the *Orchelimum*, nor as continuous; but it has the same hissing quality. The notes of *Melanoplus femur-rubrum* are irregular in length. Every grasshopper has his own song; *

Wing of Œ. niveus from life.

---

* Scudder says that these insects stridulate in four different ways, viz.:

First. By rubbing the base of one wing cover upon another, using for that purpose the veins running through the middle portion of the wing. This method includes the common crickets and the tree crickets.

Second. By a similar method, but using the veins of the inner part of the wing. This method includes the green or long-horned grasshoppers.

Third. By rubbing the inner surface of the hind legs against the notes of no two species are exactly alike, so if we will listen attentively to an occasional individual song which comes to our ears from the border of the field, we can at least be sure what kind of a creature it is which sings.

I must not omit to class among the meadow singers the grasshopper sparrow, or yellow-winged sparrow (*Ammodramus Savannarum passerinus*), sometimes wrongly called the Savannah sparrow. This bird has the remarkable gift of imitation to such a degree that we can scarcely distinguish his zigging, continuous note from

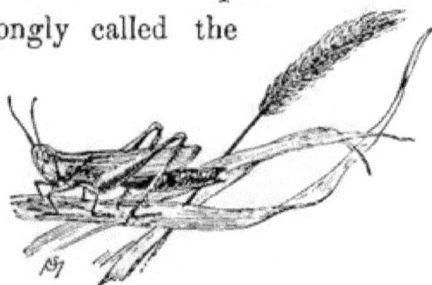
Short-winged Locust.

that of the *Orchelimum*. His crown is black with a stripe of light dull yellow through the center; his back is streaked with black, brown, red, and ashy gray, and on his shoulders are edgings of yellow.

The yellow-winged sparrow nests upon the ground, and lays four or five gray-white eggs

---

the outer surface of the wing covers. This method includes certain locusts or short-horned jumping grasshoppers.

Fourth. By rubbing together the upper surface of the front edge of the wings and the under surface of the wing covers. This method includes the locusts which stridulate during flight.

speckled with brown. Very frequently this bird appears on the grassy roadside, where it flits about shyly in and out among the weeds and the ferns, every other moment indulging in the peculiar, unmusical " sissing " note.

CHAPTER VII.

THE attempt to convey by note to any one an idea of musical sound different from what is generally accepted as music I realize is a questionably useful task; but in my estimation it is the only practical way of recording those familiar sounds of Nature which all of us should school ourselves to know and trace to their proper source. I would suggest, therefore, to those who unfortunately can not read music, to refer the bird songs to some musical member of the family, who, with the aid of the piano, will solve the enigmatical characters and thus produce a close imitation of bird melody.

The best thing to know about a bird is his song; and this can undoubtedly be recorded with perfect accuracy by musical signs; but *tone* it is not possible to record, especially if it is broken into quarter-tones and eighth-tones. This is exactly what the bird does, and consequently it is extremely difficult to know whether he means to sing A or A sharp, or whether, on account of a facile change in the quality of his note, he means to sing A at all! But, on the other hand, there is no denying it, the bird sings distinctly a minor or a major third, and also fifths and octaves, and not infrequently a good bit of the chromatic scale. This simply means that the bird sings conventional music, and we are justified in recording it with conventional musical signs.

Wagner's bird song in Siegfried is nothing more musical than an American thrush can perform; the thirds are true to the thrush's idea of music. I place the notes here for comparison with the song of the hermit thrush :

Compare this with the notes which I have recorded farther on (in Chapter X), belonging to the hermit, and estimate which would be the more difficult bit for the mocking bird to learn! But the imitative music of a bird is artificial and only interesting because it is remarkable and curious. The natural song of any bird is sweeter and more lovely by far than the bald whistle notes it can be taught to imitate. A bull-

finch, once a great pet in our family, had been
trained to sing this:
But, true to the
bird instinct of
melody, he ren-
dered the last note B instead of A and slurred it to G.

The little yellowbird in his double chirp "slurs"
with even greater distinctness,
as follows :
But the happy little creature
that says "*chee-ep*" exactly like
the canary also sings on the wing, and repeats the
slur with still greater emphasis. He dips along in
graceful undulations, high up in the air — up and
down, up and down
— and on each recov-
ery sings joyfully
thus :

The yellowbird, it is safe to say, does the same
thing the world over at sundown; and when we see

Flight of the Yellowbird.

him in company with the night hawk (only several
hundred feet below him), skimming the blue sky

which arches the Pemigewasset Valley in New Hampshire, we may be sure he will very soon be performing the same antics four hundred miles away among the hills of Pennsylvania.

I never see or hear the little fellow without thinking of that line in the old familiar hymn which runs:

Or if on joyful wing cleaving the skies.

It is almost impossible to pass along the highway at about seven o'clock in the evening of a fine midsummer's day without seeing or hearing the yellowbird as he flits chirping along overhead.

But I must also introduce another rendering of the yellowbird's song, as it is given by Mr. Simeon Pease Cheney. Here it is:*

Mr. Cheney also says that a very similar description of this bird's song he had seen from the pen of Mr. Burroughs. What I wish particularly to emphasize in this matter of bird singing is the fact that it is perfectly possible by means of musical signs to identify the bird's song beyond a shadow of doubt. †

---

* It is from one of a number of perfectly delightful articles on bird music, by Mr. Simeon Pease Cheney. I advise every one who loves birds to read them. See the Century Magazine for June, 1889.

† My own experience eight years ago will prove this. Upon

THE LURGAN ROAD,
DELAWARE VALLEY,
BUCK'S CO., PA.

THE YELLOWBIRD.

It is somewhat disappointing not to find in Wilson's American Ornithology any adequate or thoroughly reliable description of the songs of birds. The great ornithologist did not know that both the hermit and the tawny thrush are great vocalists. Even Elliot Coues has very little to say about their songs.

Wilson speaks of the yellowbird's song as weakly resembling that of the English goldfinch; he also says that at sunrise, when great numbers of yellowbirds assemble on the same tree to bask and dress themselves, "the confused mingling of their notes forms a kind of harmony not at all unpleasant." This is exactly the character of bird music which, as I have pointed out, is inadequately expressed by notes. But if I should attempt to write out this morning song it would run somewhat thus:

The first four notes are simply two introductory "cheeps," and the rest are very canarylike.

Every one ought to know the yellowbird, or

glancing over the articles on bird music, by Mr. Cheney, in the Century, I instantly recognized among his musical interpretations the songs of the hermit thrush, Wilson's thrush, scarlet tanager, and yellowbird.

goldfinch (*Spinus tristis*), by sight. The top of its head, its wings, and tail are black ; all the rest of the body is canary-yellow except beneath, where it is whitish ; the bill and legs are cinnamon-brown. This is the costume of the male bird during the summer : in winter the yellow assumes an olive tinge, more nearly like the dull hues of the female. These birds build a nest pretty well up among the twigs of the gray birch, the red cherry, or the wild apple ; in it are laid four or five dull-white eggs, daintily speckled brown. If one wishes to hear the yellow-bird's song at its best he must rise at about half past four on a clear June morning ; at this hour the sparrows, finches, robins, and meadow larks are all singing at once—a regular medley of musical tones with never a pause between ! I will not attempt the impossible task of writing out this matutinal symphony, but a good title of it in plain English has been given to us by Robert Louis Stevenson in his Child's Garden of Verses :

Ain't you 'shamed, you sleepy-head !

The greatest singers, by far (at least of New England), are the sparrows. But there are so many different species that I can only describe two or three which seem to be the commonest. Chief among these is the song sparrow (*Melospiza fasciata*). He is mainly responsible for the great disturbance of public peace at sunrise. Wilson calls him the earliest, sweetest, and most lasting songster of all, and he is quite correct in this estimate if only the silvery voiced thrushes are not included. He is a little longer or slimmer than the English sparrow, but browner in color, and pretty well flecked over the breast and sides with pointed spots of dark brown. The ashen color about eye and chin are not nearly so pronounced in this species as it is on the chipping sparrow and the tree sparrow. He is also a larger and a browner bird than the field sparrow, and as the neck and whole breast of the swamp sparrow are ash-color he bears only slight resemblance to this bird.

Song Sparrow.

He sings all summer long and well on into the fall, and we may see him at almost any hour of the day or evening perched on the topmost twig of a tree pouring forth his music with all the variety and execution of a canary. He also has a happy fashion of sing-

9

ing to himself—*sotto voce*—as he flits among the shrubbery near the ground searching for seeds. His music is spontaneous and variable, and he is entitled to be called the musician *par excellence* of the meadow. Many of his notes, though, are similar to those of the yellowbird and the indigo bird, but the scope of his voice is greater than either of these two sweet singers; the following is a characteristic example:

It will be noticed that his song generally ends with a trill, but not always, for I have heard him in the morning sing thus:

Another song which I heard while wandering through the Arnold arboretum, on March 22d last, ran in this wise:

MUSKINGUM DRIVE,
MARIETTA,
WASHINGTON CO.,
OHIO.

THE CHIPPING
SPARROW.

The song sparrows build their nests on the ground or near it in a low dense bush. In the nest there are usually four or five little white eggs, sometimes of a blue-gray tone, plentifully freckled with rusty-red spots; the birds often raise more than one brood in a season. The plumage of the female is scarcely different from that of the male.

As for the pert, little chipping sparrow (*Spizella socialis*), I believe he commonly lives on the highway, and not very far, either, from some habitation. He is, in truth, a sociable little creature who will thankfully pick up as many crumbs as are spread for him. I gave a little fellow his choice one morning of some fat young cut worms and bits of dry bread. He chose the latter and spurned the former, much to my surprise, although from my own point of view the worms were repulsive; but between worms and crumbs one would naturally think the bird's choice would fall on the former.

The chipping sparrow, I think, has no musical voice; the best he can do in the way of singing is to utter a monotonous "chip," and a continuous, crescendo *ch-ch-ch-ch-ch-ch-ch-ch-ch-ch-ch-chip*. But he is a familiar character, often seen flitting along the roadside among the stalks of goldenrod in summer time, and, later on in the season, helping himself to the seeds of the hardhack (*Spiræa tomentosa*). He is strongly marked about the head and wings with chestnut-brown and a blackish brown; above and beneath his eye are long lines of ashen-gray, and his breast is also this color. The female is similarly but less darkly colored; she lays four or five light-blue eggs. The nest is usually built in the bushes beside some brook that passes beneath the road.

The yellow-winged sparrow has been described in the foregoing chapter on Meadow Singers.

The field sparrow (*Spizella pusilla*) is another small character with a red-brown head, a bit gray over the eye, brown back, streaked black, edged with gray, and an

Field Sparrow.

ocher-colored breast; the bill is reddish light brown. He has a good loud voice of his own, and I am by no means sure that he ever subsides to the cricket-like chirrup such as Wilson describes. His song is restricted to perhaps three tones, but these are *distinctly* musical :

The first three notes are given with deliberation, then he hurries on and finishes with a loud canary-like, chirruping trill. Mr. Minot speaks of his "exquisitely modulated whistles," but this is not a strictly accurate description, for the first three notes are alike, and are given with unmistakable accent and without the slightest modulation.* It is amusing to watch the little bird as he stands on the low, projecting bough of a yellow birch and repeats his simple song over and over again at intervals of about twelve seconds (it only occupies five). Each time he sings he tips his head backward and a trifle sideways, and throws his voice out with all his might, ending in an almost imperceptible, high grace note on which he shuts his bill very unceremoniously; then, perhaps, he shifts his position a trifle, scrapes his bill on the branchlet, which, I presume, is equivalent to clearing his throat, and proceeds as before. In another instant he is two hundred yards away, down in the meadow border, singing the same song again.†

---

* I hardly agree with Mr. Cheney, however, that this sparrow's song is confined to a minor third; but most likely all field sparrows do not sing alike.

† His song is not invariably like that which I have given; sometimes he indulges in a simple short trill. I chose the particular song recorded, because it coincided to a remarkable degree with one written by Mr. Cheney; which fact is conclusive evidence that *Spizella pusilla* was the bird undoubtedly heard in both instances.

The field sparrow's nest is usually on the ground; it is built of coarse grasses, rootlets, and bits of weed stalks. The eggs (from three to four) are white marked with red-brown specks.

A really tame bird, and one which is a trifle troublesome about a cottage in the woods, is the Phœbe, sometimes called pewit or pewee (*Sayornis Phœbe*). This little creature sometimes prefers to build her nest under the eaves of my piazza or woodshed, and there is much ado to protect the young from the enemy, a pet Manx cat. But one fine morning Mr. Manx succeeded in passing an extemporized barricade and devoured the whole family—not a small matter, as Mrs. Phœbe usually raises five little ones.

The Phœbe generally builds her nest under the span of some bridge, using mud, sticks, hairs, bits of rag, or, in fact, anything convenient, no matter what its nature; in the nest we will probably find five white eggs sparingly dotted on the larger ends with rusty-red. I have drawn with the phœbe that picturesque bridge crossing the Clinton River, Pontiac, Mich.

I can not say that the bird is a pretty one, but it is at least softly colored. The head, which is somewhat crested, is black; the back is rusty-black, and the breast is sooty-white—almost gray. The two colors meet on a line at the eye, giving the bird a

CLINTON RIVER,
PONTIAC, OAKLAND CO.,
MICH.

PHŒBE BIRD.

fine-appearing, characteristic head. As the male bird sits on a branch of the apple tree near the nest he sings his one song of only two notes, thus:

Sometimes he hiccoughs in the finale, thus: "*Phœ-hick-be*."

But the song is quite monotonous and sounds remarkably like some thin, piping voice calling for "Phœbe." In size the bird is a trifle larger than the song sparrow. He holds a nearly *upright* position as he sits on a twig, and now and then suddenly darts after some passing insect, but returns immediately to resume his song. He cocks his head this way and that as he sits and sings, evidently keeping a sharp lookout for stray millers, flies, and bees.

CHAPTER VIII.

THERE are quite a number of birds whose unmusical voices are frequently heard along the highway, and whose emphatic and curiously expressive notes are nearly as interesting as the songs of more skillful singers.

It is not perfectly just, however, to use the term *unmusical* in connection with *any* of the voices of Nature, but I employ the word here in a comparative sense. An acute ear will detect the musical quality in every sound; the unmusical ear is simply more or less tone-deaf. He who sings so simple a melody as My Country 'tis of thee, and "flats" without knowing it, lacks the ability to measure the *intervals between the tones*; he could never make a pianoforte tuner! How much less, then, can we expect him to discover the distinct musical fifth in the distant bellow of a cow on the hillside : *

* Not all cows bellow thus, but a great many come exceedingly close to this description.

120

In any sound of whatever kind which is not a harsh noise, there is a keynote (tone). Niagara Falls is no exception to the rule; to my ear it distinctly hums a profound organ note. But according to atmospheric conditions and one's relative position to the falls, the organ tone is higher or lower.

We can not pass a barn yard without hearing the unmusical cackle of the hen; yet a little careful attention will perhaps bring with it the knowledge that the racket is not simply a noise after all. This is what I make of it:

Not even the twitting chatter of the barn swallow is really unmusical, and the night song of a million crickets is a lullaby of two soothing notes,* immensely musical in effect.

It is the case, then, that there are unmusical birds, if we consider the matter strictly in the light of com-

---

* See Chapter VI, Meadow Singers.

parison. The hermit thrush is a musician, but the little chipping sparrow has no music in his soul beyond what we may discover in his lisping *chip*. Some of the birds have most remarkably vigorous voices, which, musical or unmusical, we are pretty sure to hear at no very great distance from the highway.

The first of these is the golden-crowned thrush (not a thrush at all but a warbler), or ovenbird (*Seiurus aurocapillus*). He is about six inches long. His back is brown-olive, his crown subdued golden-orange edged by black stripes, his breast and sides are streaked with black, and his under parts are dull white.

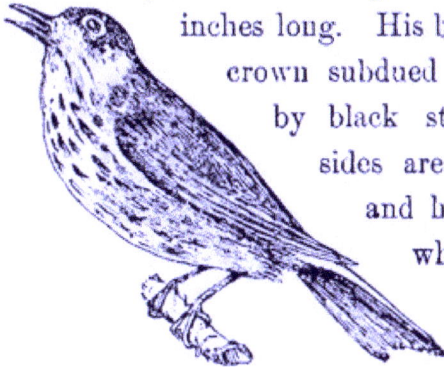

The golden-crowned thrush has an emphatic and some-what hysterical voice, which slightly resembles the loud swishing sound of a stout whip as it is lashed back and forth. What he says seems to be:

Golden-crowned Thrush.

"Queecher, Queecher, QUEECHER, QUEECHER, QUEECHER, QUEECHER."

But although these notes are far from musical, they

possess a strong *whistlelike* quality which is at least startling and amusing.*

Burrough's interpretation of this bird's language is " *Teacher, teacher,*" etc., crescendo, fortissimo. This loud-voiced golden-crowned thrush has also a fine melodic warble which he indulges in about the time of sunset during the nesting season; but his summer note, the only one I know, is the far more common *queecher*.

The nest is usually built on the ground in the woods; in it one may find from three to four white eggs marked with rust-color and brown on the larger ends.

The next bird with an unmusical note is the Maryland yellowthroat (*Geothlypis trichas*). This modest little creature is scarcely more than five inches long. His back, wings, and tail are dull olive-green; over the forehead and about the eyes is a broad band of slate-black edged above by another band of white; the throat and breast are yellow and the legs silver-white.

The nest † is built in some secluded retreat among

---

* I can not with satisfaction locate the tone; I should say it was a presto slur back and forth between the third E above and the fourth B above middle C.

† The nest is rarely found: but Burroughs describes his good fortune in discovering it one day about six inches from the ground, in a bunch of ferns. It was a massive nest built of the

the briers, dead leaves, and grass, on or very near the
ground; in it the little bird lays from three to five
tiny, semitranslucent, buff-white eggs speckled with
reddish brown.

Maryland Yellowthroat.

Among the moun-
tain maples beside the
road, and often through
the alder thickets which
border the brook, the
yellowthroat may be
seen flitting here and
there, and occasionally
stopping to inquire —
"*Which* is it? *Which* is it? *Which* is it?" in a
shrill, piping voice; or frequently he seems to say
" *We*-chi-chi-chee. *We*-chi-chi-chee. *We*-chi-chi-
chee." *

The Maryland yellowthroat is a regular visitor
of Campton, N. H. Throughout the glad months
of May and June he is perpetually dodging in and
out among the shrubbery of the beautiful highway
that leads northward to the Franconia Notch, and

stalks and leaves of dried grass, and lined with fine, dark-brown
roots.

* Frank M. Chapman, in the Handbook of Birds, says: "The
birds near New York city seem to me to say, 'I beseech you, I
beseech you, I beseech you,' though, to be sure, the tone is far
from pleading."

HURON RIVER,
NEAR ANN ARBOR,
WASHTENAW CO.,
MICH.

THE CHICKADEE.

continuously pressing the passers-by with his vigorous questioning.

Another unmusical character, and a quite common
one, is the black-capped titmouse, or chickadee (*Parus
atricapillus*). This bird is a little over five inches
long. His head is black and the rest of his body is
in effect a pretty even gray; beneath and behind his
eye is a well-marked, wedge - shaped gray - white
band; the throat is black and the breast white-
gray; the wings and tail are blackish but gray-
edged.

The titmouse chooses for a nest some hole in a
tree, and Wilson says the bird not infrequently is
satisfied with the deserted retreat of a squirrel or a
woodpecker. According to my own observations
the titmice sometimes return to their own previous
home, and continue housekeeping again as though
they had never been away. For two years past
apparently the same pair of birds have come back
to the old home in an apple tree behind my cottage.
The female lays five or six white eggs speckled with
brown-red.

These birds are characteristically vivacious. They
are veritable little acrobats, forever tumbling about
the small twigs of the orchard trees, now upside down
and again letting go their hold to turn (it always
looks that way) a double back somersault in the

air! Hardly is this performance ended when two twittering individuals engage in a momentary "scrap," and away they flit to a neighboring tree. Then a sprightly, rasping little voice is heard, saying: " *Chick-a-dee-dee-dee-dee !* *Chick-a-dee-dee-dee !* " The " *chick* " is a squeaky whistle, and the " *dee-dee* " is a rasping, flat note like that of the blue jay. To my ear it has a nasal quality. I have drawn this bird in one of his characteristic positions. He frequents the river borders where the trees and bushes bend over the water, so I have sketched with him a bit of the pretty Huron River, near Ann Arbor, Mich., where he can frequently be seen flitting in and out among the shrubbery.

A still more familiar bird, whose nest is pretty sure to be among the alders or the elder-berry bushes, not far from the highway, is the catbird (*Galeoscoptes Carolinensis*), a not very distant relative of the musical thrush. He is almost a uniform slate-gray, his crown and tail being but a trifle blacker; under his tail and wings is a dark ruddy color. The nest will be found firmly fixed in the crotch of an elder-berry bush, maybe, and in it we will see from three to five *deep* blue-green eggs without spots. Near by the female is restlessly bobbing in and out among the foliage, flirting her tail and inviting us to move on. I recollect from early boyhood just such a nest, situ-

ated exactly this way in a certain wooded lot near
the road which led down to one of the most beautiful sheets of water in Putnam County, N. Y.—Lake
Mahopac.

We are aware of the proximity of a catbird by
the sudden note of uneasiness which we hear. The
sound is certainly very catlike, but harsh and hoarse!
The catbird's notes are devoid of sonorous quality;
one is a snappy *trut-tut-tut-tut-tut*, and another is
a flat and nasal mew which starts loud and suddenly
and finishes with a diminuendo, thus:

$$sf\ldots\ldots\ldots\ldots dim.$$

$$\text{`` B---}^{ja-\ \ a-}_{\quad a-a-aa.}\text{'' }*$$

However similar this may be to the cat's mce-ow, I do
not think it is nearly as much like it as the screech of
the peacock, who really does say

$$\text{`` Mee-}^{yow-}_{\quad ow-}{}_{ow-w-w}\text{''}$$

with unmistakable distinctness, and *double fortissimo*
too! Truth to tell, the peacock can out-yowl the cat
on all occasions.

The catbird, however, is not unmusical; his mew
is perhaps his only rasping note, for when he chooses
to sing at the time of nesting, more particularly in

---

* The a as in jasper.

the early morning, his notes are extremely varied and expressive. Here are some of them :

softly.

We-o   We-o   /jay\   spink-ink-wheo-e - ah - - - gee-z-z-z-z-Z whir-r

But whether he is nearly related to the thrushes or not, the fact remains that his songs are neither of silver nor of gold ; and, figuratively speaking, these precious metals *are* melted into music as soon as the hermit and the Wilson thrushes open their throats !

This reminds me of the fact that the voices of birds are more varied and musical than those of any other creatures in the world. Even the rooster has a tuneful crow—

The cat tribe roars and mews and hisses ; that is all. But the birds !—is there any end to their powers of vocaliza-

Cock - a - doo-dle do.

tion ? They can chirrup, chip, caw, whip-poor-will, whistle, chick-a-dee, hoot, howl, cackle, crow, gobble, quack, drum, cluck, chirp like crickets, mew like cats, talk like human beings, cry like babies, squeak like cart wheels ; in fine, beyond their own extensive *répertoire* of musical and unmusical sounds, they

can (many of them) imitate all creation from the
voice of man down to a creaking barn door!

Three of the strangest of the bird voices (they are
also very familiar ones) are those of the whip-poor-

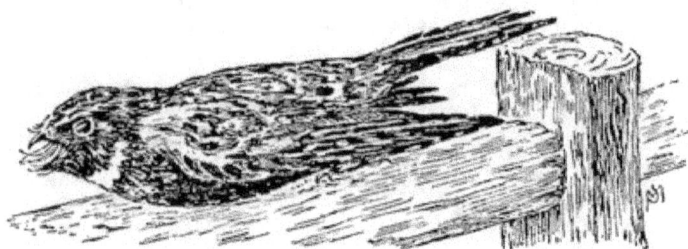

Whip-poor-will.

will, night hawk, and screech owl. The first every
one recognizes, and the uncanny tones of the last
probably every one knows without being able to tell
what kind of a creature they belong to. Both of
these birds are, in a measure, musical, although it
will be difficult for me to represent by musical signs
the true character of their singing. As every one, I
suppose, can recall the exact intonation of the whip-
poor-will's few notes, I imagine it will be interesting
to see how they can be musically rendered :

The "kuk" we can only hear if we are within
10

twenty yards or so of the bird ; it sounds as though in sucking in his breath for the next "whip" he snapped his beak together. This somewhat melancholy vesper song begins at sundown and continues, less and less frequently, well on into the night. The whip-poor-will (*Antrostomus vociferus*) is a large bird, perhaps ten inches long. About his bill are long, stiff, curved hairs. His colors are a variety of tawny, light, and dark browns ; on the breast is a narrow band of white. In this respect his coloring is exactly like that of a toad, or perhaps the large brown branch of a tree on which he sits in a crouching attitude, with his wings slightly spread and his body jerking violently with every "whip."

The bird is not often seen, but he is heard everywhere, and one can locate him by the sound of his voice, now on the wood pile,* then on the fence, next in the copse beside the road, and again in the bushes bordering the garden. Before one knows it he is gone ; he flies low and silently, and sails along until he reaches, some thirty yards away, a convenient

---

* I think it is Dr. Abbott who has intimated that the wood pile has of late years gone out of fashion as a perch for the whip-poor-will. That may be the case in civilized New Jersey : but should any one come up into the wilds of New Hampshire and sit on an obscure corner of my wood pile at dusk, I think he will be convinced that the whip-poor-will has not given up his old habit !

bough, upon which he settles and immediately begins his song again.

The whip-poor-will does not build a nest, but selects some very secluded spot in the woods, where, among the brush, dry leaves, and old logs, she usually lays two eggs resembling those of the night hawk, of a dull gray-white color spotted plentifully with olive-brown. It is a common but curious practice among some birds *not* to build nests, but either to depend upon those of other birds or to take all the chances of harm to their offspring by choosing a merely sequestered spot on the ground.

The next strange-voiced bird is the night hawk (*Chordeiles Virginianus*). A strange-looking creature (not a true hawk at all), with a very small bill and a very large mouth, closely resembling the whip-poor-will, but far more beautifully marked. The night hawk is about ten inches long; around his eyes is a buffish brown patch bounded below with a triangular patch of dull white, which extends beneath the bill; the wings and tail are blackish brown with sharply defined bands of dull white; the other parts are varied tones of spotted light brown.

The female has no band of white about the throat, and is very moderately marked on wings and tail. She lays two eggs of a gray-white tone, speckled all over with olive-brown, in some secluded spot by the edge of the wood; the eggs so closely resemble the general color-effect of dried leaves, stones, and brown ground that they are hard to discover. Of course the birds build no nests. It is a peculiarity of the night hawk that by reason of the short and slender form of his legs and feet, which are in no wise adapted to grasp a limb crosswise with any firmness, he sits on the branch *lengthwise*. This is also the case with the whip-poor-will; I have never seen either bird in any other position on fence rail or tree.

About the twilight hour the performances of the night hawk on the wing are most extraordinary; it is not possible for one to miss seeing them in summer time, while passing along the highway just after sunset. Far above valley and hill he circles, a small bird in appearance (although in reality he measures twenty-three inches across with his wings spread). Slowly and quietly he continues an erratic flight, with apparently no object in view except that of enjoying a little exercise, and uttering the while his shrill whistled "geep, geep, geep" (not unlike the squeaking of a cart wheel). Suddenly we see him pitch over head foremost and fall precipitately seventy or eighty feet as though shot; but he recovers himself immediately and rises to greater heights. Hardly is the recovery complete, however, before a strange whirr-r-r-r-rrr, reaches our ears, sounding perhaps like the *very* distant bellow of a cow forsaken on some lonely hillside. The sound has a sonorous quality which it is hard to describe. I have heard a fractious rolling door make just such a noise, and in a sudden rise from the ground the pigeon makes a weaker but similar one by the rapid beating of the air with his wings.* Wilson says the same sound may be produced by blowing strongly into the bunghole of an empty hogshead, but he adds that the night hawk doubtlessly makes this noise by the sudden expansion of his capacious mouth while he passes through

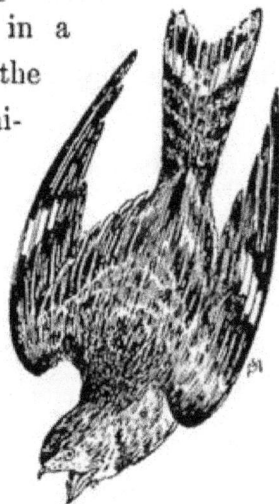

The Night Hawk's tumble.

the air! (What an extraordinary theory!) I am sure that the rapid beating of the bird's wings to recover himself after his swift fall is the most satisfactory explanation of the mysterious "whirr-r-r-r-rrr." †

---

* I must not omit to say, too, that the partridge, at the end of his "drumming," also whirrs.

† This is Audubon's theory. But I do not entertain the slightest doubt about the matter. The sound reaches the ear just after the recovery, and this is of itself an all-sufficient proof that the wings produce it; nevertheless it is said that the European goat-

The last strange-voiced creature is the oddest of all; it is the screech owl (*Megascops asio*), a blood-thirsty little villain, scarcely eight inches tall as he sits on a bough; nevertheless he sings. His colors are brown and gray, and they are pretty well mixed. In some specimens which I have seen the coloring is decidedly ruddy; but this is not to be wondered at as the birds are extremely variable in the general tone of their plumage. The screech owl makes her nest in the hollow trunk of a tree; it is, of course, a very slight affair, of much the same character as a hen's nest, with bits of grass, feathers, shreds of bark, and so forth, in its make up. The eggs are white, clean, and nearly round in form; there are from three to five in a nest.

I said the owl sang; but I must admit that the song is not altogether musical, for it has yet another far more ascendant quality. There is something eerie about its cadence, something depressing about its unearthly sadness, which on a dark night makes one's flesh creep! We might take it for the despairing, quavering voice of a lost and wandering spirit, or the distant ghostly cheers of Henrick Hudson's

---

sucker utters the hollow whirr when perched and while holding his head downward. I doubt it, though. Frank M. Chapman, I am glad to say, considers that the night hawk's whirr is produced by the passage of air through the bird's primaries, i. e., larger wing feathers.

DIXVILLE NOTCH,
COOS CO,
NEW HAMPSHIRE.

THE SCREECH OWL.

crew up in the mountain, when some one of their number has made a "ten strike."

The song of the screech owl may be musical or not, that is a matter of opinion ; but that it is a great stimulant to the imagination there can be no possible shadow of doubt!   We perhaps think of all manner of blood-curdling things which may be happening, and the suggestive voice fits the case exactly ; in fact, we might find ourselves wondering why we do not fly to the rescue !

Here is a peculiarly distressing crescendo shake which is quite common :

It is just a little bit suggestive of a tree

'Ah...

toad, yet it is not the quiet, subdued voice of that soothing little creature at all.   Again, the owl sings : and we imagine some one badly hurt lying moaning

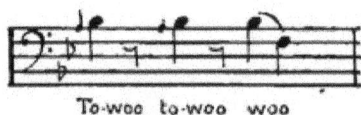

To-woo to-woo woo

and nearly breathless on the distant road.   But again we hear the strange voice, and now it sounds like a far - away hysterical laugh : *This* is the owl's spring song !

Ah! Ah! Ah!

The screech owl is a bird of prey, and he is not

particular about a small matter of theft and murder; for some night he will appear before the oriole's home when the family is asleep, and if the nest in the pear tree is shallow he will claw out the young ones and devour them at his leisure one by one. Not even the mother bird may escape his murderous attack. The pendulous nest of the oriole is comparatively safe in either the elm or the maple, because on both these trees the leaves are large and abundant; but in spring the orchard trees with their thin foliage are bad homes for birds and good hunting grounds for owls. However, the chief food of this owl is mice and insects; he does not often dine on young orioles.

The screech owl is common North and South. He flits at dusk along the roads which wind through the mountains of northern New Hampshire, and he resorts to the unfrequented byways of New Jersey; in fact, he is a bird quite at home on the dark and lonely road, where he can undisturbed plan his mischievous plots—robber that he is! I have met him in the far North on the shaded road which approaches the Dixville Notch, N. H., and on a lonely byway leading through the scrubby pines of Monmouth County, N. J.

CHAPTER IX.

BIRDS OF BRILLIANT FEATHERS—HUMMING BIRD, JAY,
BLUEBIRD, TANAGER, ORIOLE, ETC.

HUMMING BIRDS have been aptly called "the
jewels of ornithology." And in truth they *are* perfect little jewels on the wing. We can only realize
this fact after having been fortunate enough to hold
one of the tiny, fairylike creatures in our hand; then
the rubies, emeralds, and sapphires show themselves
in all their astonishing, miniature beauty. The remarkable "gorget" (for so the humming bird's ruby
collar is named) under a magnifying glass is a blaze
of resplendent red fire! The subtile color is far
more beautiful than that which we see in the ruby;
in proof of which hold the magnifying glass close
to a spinel ruby and note its glassy lifelessness in
comparison. John Ruskin was quite right when he
said that there was far more preciousness of color in
rainbows, dewdrops, and birds' wings than in diamonds

137

and rubies.* It is well worth while to examine a peacock's tail feather under the glass; what burning hues are there! Gold and copper, emerald green and cerulean blue, violet and ultramarine, purple, yellow, and even such remarkable tints as lilac and aquamarine green (these last are on the extreme outer edge of the broad, copper-colored field, in the center of which is the emerald-rimmed violet eye). We can not see the lilac and green without the glass, nor without its aid can we appreciate the jewel-beauty of the tiny little " hummer." He is all golden - green above, with wings of dusky violet, and breast of dull pearly white ; but his red collar is the most remarkable part of his coloring.

The Rubythroat.

The beautiful little rubythroat humming bird (*Trochilus colubris*) belongs to a very large family; he represents one of no less than five hundred spe-

---

* In the Lectures on Art he says, after praising the plumage of the peacock and kingfisher: " Entirely common and vulgar compared with these . . . we have the colors of gems. The green of the emerald is the best of these, but at its best is as vulgar as house-painting beside the green of bird's plumage or of clear water. . . . The ruby is like the pink of an ill-dyed and half-washed-out print compared to the dianthus."

cies of hummers, most of which have been positively specified.* Fifteen distinct species are common in the United States.

Humming birds, I might add, are peculiarly American ; but they are mostly confined to the tropical portions of the southern continent, particularly to the United States of Colombia and Brazil. Our own little rubythroat is comparatively small beside the largest and most magnificent species but recently discovered in Arizona, named *Eugenes fulgens*. This gorgeous hummer is something like six inches in length! I believe he stands number four hundred and eight on the list.

We must not be disappointed if among more than half the little hummers that we see the ruby color is quite wanting. The female does not wear a red collar, but she has the same golden-green back and purple wings, although, perhaps, these are not quite as brilliant as those of her mate.† The tongue of the humming bird is, I think, the most remarkable part of its anatomy; it is like a double-barreled

---

* It seems strange that Wilson knew of only this one species. It is astounding to learn that within the eighty odd years succeeding his time nearly four hundred new species have been discovered, and *over* four hundred specifically labeled !

† There are other differences, too : the tail of the male is forked, that of the female is double-scallop-shaped with black bars, and lateral feathers white-tipped.

shotgun, only instead of belching forth murderous shot, it sucks in the sweets of the flowers. This extraordinary little double-tubed tongue is guided into the honeysuckle's long throat by well-developed, strong muscles; and while the bee is vainly bustling about, plunging his head "up to his ears" in the aggravating blossom all to no purpose, our little hummer makes one lightinglike dart at it and secures the honey with apparently no effort whatever.

I find the humming bird is very fond of nasturtiums, petunias, and delphiniums, and notwithstanding the fact that the milkweed blossom is cloyingly sweet, he passes it by, where it stands just beside the road near my garden fence, and makes a bee line for my brilliant, red King of Tom Thumbs and my ruby-spotted yellow Ladybird nasturtiums. Perhaps he does not fancy the æsthetic, lilac-drab colors of the ubiquitous milkweed.

The little fellow has mere apologies for legs; they are quite useless for locomotion, but are admirably adapted for a tiny perch. He can support himself firmly on a wire scarcely thicker than a hairpin. He stands on the wire screening which supports my sweet peas—very light wire it is, too—and preens his feathers with every appearance of security and contentment. While he is at the flowers feeding he utters a short, nervous "chip, chip," as though he were not quite sure that some one would not take advantage of his position and catch him by the tail.

There is no bird that can build a nest as soft and beautiful as that of the humming bird. It is a tiny affair, about an inch and a quarter broad inside, lined with bits of cotton, soft hairs, and moss, and covered outside with patches of lichens. The nest usually contains two white, pearly eggs (I believe the humming bird never lays more than two). It is a curious fact that it is most frequently planted solidly on a good-sized horizontal bough, and looks more like a lichen-covered excrescence on the latter than it does like a bird's nest.

The little rubythroat is not as wild and timid as might be supposed. If we are patient and quiet he will often perch very near us, and if we have a bunch of flowers in our hand, make bold enough to approach and help himself to their sweets.

It is nonsense to suppose that only a few possess the knack of becoming the intimate friends of wild birds and animals; if there is such a thing as a gift of this nature it is a very commonplace, practical one, composed of tact and patience rather than sentiment. The squirrel will run across our toes if it suits his convenience, and the bird will take crumbs from our hand if he is hungry enough; all depends upon our own patience and willingness to stand or sit still for an indefinite period. As there are many restless people who can not do this, I am inclined to believe that they are the only ones who never can become the favored friends of squirrels and birds. It is doubtful, however, whether even inanimate stones are counted as friends by the wary crow—that steely blue-black * beauty of the cornfield. He is a cynic of the bird family, suspicious of everything and everybody, to whom the merest novelty (no matter what its nature) is part of a plot for his destruction. A dozen or so of four-foot sticks, connected by harmless lines of white twine, placed here and there in the cornfield, are, according to his way of thinking, a substantial menace to public safety—that is, the safety of the tribe, *Corvus Americanus*. But the crow is wily ; he is sagacious beyond calculation, and he fully understands the value of sentinel duty. Before we can get within gunshot of the ten maranders which we see are plainly engaged in " hoeing the farmer's corn," a sharp signal " caw-r-rrr " comes from the edge of the copse near by—the game is up, and the birds are flown !

The crow's nest is a rough affair, built high up in

---

* The beautiful iridescent black of the crow's feathers is no ordinary color ; its brilliancy is unattainable so far as the artist's paint box is concerned.

the tree; it contains from four to six generally blue-green (rarely white) eggs speckled brown.

There is another bird, not so distant a relative of the crow either, who when he is hungry does not hesitate to help himself from a plate of food, accidently exposed in the preparation of a meal in camp, or even from a hand holding an enticing crust. This is the Canada jay (*Perisoreus Canadensis*), a bright, quaker-drab-colored, gray-

Canada Jay.

vested, white-breasted individual, as bold as his crow cousin is wary. He is a large bird, eleven inches in length, with wing feathers mostly white-tipped; I first became acquainted with him on the summit of Mount Osceola, one of the southern peaks of the White Mountains, situated in Waterville. Here, several years ago, in midsummer, while my companion and myself were resting and refreshing ourselves with our luncheon, we fed three Canada jays from our hands. So greedy was one of them that he crammed two fair-sized crusts in his bill and endeavored to seize the third; one of his feet rested in my palm and the other grasped my thumb. Several tree sparrows (*Spizella monticola*) near by also seemed anxious to have a share of the feast, but no quietude nor persuasiveness of manner on our part sufficiently encouraged them to feed from our hands; they would fly quite near, and one even ventured to snatch a crumb from off my knee. Rarely the Canada jay has appeared down in the valley near my cottage, probably with a view of filching some tidbits around by the kitchen way. He has a hoarse voice similar to that of the blue jay, but not so boisterous; sometimes he gives a low, nervous whistle. The nest is usually found in a spruce tree; it contains from four to five white eggs speckled with light olive-brown.

The Canada jay has a cousin who is decked in far finer feathers; this is the blue jay (*Cyanocitta cristata*); he is also related to the crow. But he is a bold creature, full of pranks and nonsense, who always creates a sensation in the bird world. His costume is a perfect "symphony in blue"; cadet blue, ultramarine, pale blue, gray, black, and white—these are his regimentals.

The blue jay's voice is a familiar one; we all

immediately recognize his catlike " ja-ja-ja, ja, jay ! "
Then, too, he has a

vehement whistle :   and another :

It is a characteristic of the blue jay that he is ever
on the move and *never* quiet when he moves; if he
leaves one apple tree for another he does so vociferously, no matter if the flight is only a matter of
ten feet.

The nest of the blue jay is usually snugly fixed
in the crotch of a tree branch fifteen feet or so above
the ground.   It is built mostly of small rootlets, and
contains from four to six brown-gray eggs marked
with rust-colored spots.

The delightful, good-natured bluebird (*Sialia
sialis*), whose azure wings flit with a charming effect
of color through the thin, budding foliage of early
April, is (excepting his blueness) more nearly like
the English robin redbreast than any of our other
birds; in fact, the early settlers of New England
called him the "blue robin."   He is a sociable little
creature, who approves of and patronizes the bird
house, and is pleased to pick up a few crumbs from
the piazza steps; he even perches on the railing with

11

an evident feeling of confidence in the good-will of mankind.

The bluebird is evenly colored with pale ultramarine from his crown to the middle of his back and wings; the brightest color is at the shoulders; under his bill is a little white, but his breast is rusty red. The long feathers of his wings and those of his tail are slate-gray tinged blue; beneath he is white. I can conceive of nothing more beautifully soft in color than the plumage of the bluebird in early spring, when the incipient green grass and the yet leafless but budding twigs of the orchard trees are but a welcome

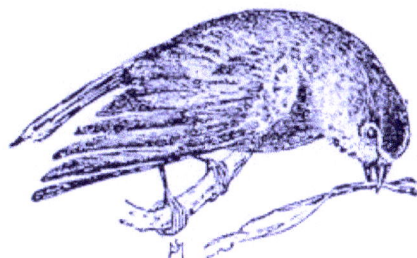

Bluebird.

promise of color to come. But if once our eyes are fortunate enough to catch the gleam of the bluebird's wings against the leaden hue of a cloudy New England sky we are satisfied ; and amid the gray surroundings the touch of cerulean blue seems as precious as it is beautiful.

It is not strange that the farmer rejoices at the advent of the bluebird, either, for it has been estimated that each pair destroys in one season from fifty to one hundred thousand worms and grubs.

The female bird is very plainly attired in brown-ish gray with only a suggestion here and there of greenish blue. She selects a bird house for her nest, or the hole in some old apple tree or fence post. Mr. Burroughs says she shows no affection for her gallant mate and no pleasure in his society, and if he is killed she goes in quest of another husband in a most businesslike manner. The nest is a simple hollow in the center of some dried grass; in it there are from four to six very pale-blue eggs.

The bluebird's song impresses me with its scrappy nature; he has only three or four notes at his command, and these are in the minor key. Like the robin, he often sings in triplets, thus:

but his notes are sweeter and not so strong; unlike the robin, though, he says very plainly as he sings:

Tre-wee, tre-wee-ly.   Tre-wee, tre-wee-ly   Tre-wee-ly, tre-wee-ly.

These notes are not like those of the canarylike yellowbird; they have a more bell-like quality. As early as the latter end of March the bluebirds begin to appear in the Arnold arboretum, near Boston, and in the township of Campton, N. H., where patches of snow still remain plentiful beside the road.

One of the most charming little birds which frequents the roadside and sings throughout August is the intensely blue indigo bunting, or indigo bird (*Passerina cyanea*). He is about five and a half inches long. The blue is an even indigo-ultramarine, darker on the head, wings (somewhat brown-tinged), and tail; indeed, it is a much *bluer* bird than the bluebird, and is perhaps more deserving of the name.*

The nest is usually built among the bushes, and in it there are generally four or five white or bluish white eggs. The male bird has a really beautiful but not strong, canarylike voice, with something of a lisping character. He sings in the top of a tree, and very frequently close beside the road. I have timed him on several occasions, and have found his song from five to seven seconds long. It generally begins with a moderate *fortissimo* and ends in a *pianissimo* trill, or sometimes with two short faint notes:

---

* The plumage, in parts, is iridescent, like that of the peacock; sometimes it appears quite greenish blue.

ROAD NEAR DODSONVILLE,
HIGHLAND CO., OHIO.

INDIGO BIRD.

But I imagine it may not be so easy to distinguish the musical indigo bird from several other chirping singers, so far as "style" is concerned, and I would advise those who are unfamiliar with the song sparrow's and the yellowbird's notes to make a careful comparison of the music of all three birds as I have represented it here. There are two or three comparisons which I can make that should aid one considerably in the attempt to distinguish these songs apart. The indigo bird's voice is sprightly, thin, irregular, and lisping, and the song lasts longer than that of the song sparrow. The latter frequently sings a tune three and a half seconds long, composed of three notes, a trill, and three strong final notes. * The indigo bird never does this. We can not divide his song into distinct parts any more than we can that of a canary; it is all one rapid medley. The yellowbird's notes can always be heard toward sunset, when the happy little fellow is on the wing, dipping along in his billowy lines of flight. This song is entirely his own, and the indigo bird never sings a single passage which remotely resembles it.

Another remarkably brilliant bird is the scarlet tanager (*Piranga erythromelas*); he is about seven inches long, and is vivid scarlet, all except his wings

---

* See the first music I have given of this sparrow in a foregoing chapter.

and tail, which are jet black. So splendid a bird, if he flies across the road from one patch of woods to another, can not fail to catch the eye on a bright day. But the flash of color is sudden and momentary— he is gone in less time than it takes to tell it! This is the male bird, though; the female is dressed in a modest costume of yellow-olive green, a splendid foil for her scarlet mate. She builds her very slight nest in an orchard tree, perhaps, and in it lays four light green - blue eggs speckled with madder brown.

Scarlet Tanager.

The scarlet tanager is most frequently heard on the edge of the wood that borders the road; he rarely comes out in the open to sing. Like the thrush he prefers the forest, but he sings a very different kind of a song. Listen: here are the notes:

Mark how much they resemble the robin's. But again we may hear another tanager sing, and we think his soft warblings are nearer like those of the Baltimore

oriole, except that the music of the latter is not soft.
It is very plain in any event that he delivers his notes
in groups of twos and threes, and this is quite characteristic of the oriole.

The scarlet tanager is, on the whole, rather a
rare bird, I think, for in my own experience he
makes a short season of it, and leaves for the
South long before the other birds do. In the Pemigewasset Valley he arrives in late May and disappears as early, I should think, as the end of September.   I never heard him sing after the middle of
June.   Wilson says his food is principally winged
insects, such as wasps, hornets, bees, and so forth.
His taste is not confined to insects, however, as he
relishes the berries which grow beside the road—
especially huckleberries. I have also noticed that he
likes the bird cherry (*Prunus Pennsylvanica*).

A rather rare brilliantly feathered bird we may
possibly see on the highway in midsummer, called
the cardinal grosbeak (*Cardinalis cardinalis*). He
is bright, light red of a pure tone, closely allied to
scarlet; the bird in captivity I have been surprised to see is greatly faded in color.   We may
know the grosbeak by his large bill, his striking crest,

which he lowers and raises at will, and his black face and throat. In song the cardinal grosbeak is not to be compared with the thrushes or the thrasher; his notes are whistled, and quite similar to those of the scarlet tanager. Very rarely I have caught sight of this beautiful bird on the wooded roadsides of New Jersey. In Virginia he is quite common.

The most brilliant bird which appears on the roadside—and he is always to be found in the elm or the maple, near some old homestead—is the Baltimore oriole* (*Icterus galbula*). He is about seven and a half inches long. His lower back and breast are brilliant orange, the head and wings are black, and a white band marks the latter. The female is olive-backed and yellow-olive-breasted. She lays about five buff-tinged white eggs marked on the larger ends with purple-brown spots. The nest is a remarkable, woven pouch, from five to seven inches deep, usually hung from an upper, slender branch. † Bits of hemp, rope, twine, hair, wool, thistle-down, or, in fact, anything shreddy which can be picked up around the house, the bird weaves into the nest with consummate skill.

---

* Named for the first Lord Baltimore because the black and orange of its plumage were the colors forming his livery.

† See also the mention of oriole nest-building on page 132.

It is often the case that the mother-bird (she most frequently does all the work) gets entangled with a bit of string while she is building the nest, and sometimes it is at the cost of her life. I have seen one bird so badly mixed up with a snarl of hair and string that her wings were helpless, and she fluttered to the ground in dangerous proximity to an ever-watchful cat; but she was rescued in time and released from the tangle. For four successive years this oriole built her nest in a sugar maple within ten feet of the hotel, and only a few yards from the highway, at Blair, N. H., where the mountain woods were near enough to satisfy birds of the most fastidious social habits; but the oriole is not content to nest farther than a dozen yards from one's doorstep.

The oriole's notes are so familiar that I do not need to give more than a few of the commoner ones to refresh our memory :

The couplets are very clear and distinct, and have a better pitch, perhaps, than those of the robin. However similarly the two birds may sing, we can

always tell one from the other by the quality of
their notes; those of the oriole are more bell-like or
liquid, but the robin's are robust, and most generally
confined to a low-pitch warble. Both, however, are
loud whistlers.

CHAPTER X.

THE plain-coated thrushes are our greatest singers.
Whoever has not heard them at the sunset hour,
while wheeling along the road in late spring or
early summer, has yet to hear the sweetest songs
of the sky.

Wilson says little or nothing about the music of
two or three singularly gifted members of the Thrush
family, and it is particularly to these that I wish to
draw attention. The *Turdidæ* is a large family ; in
one subdivision alone (the *Turdinæ*) there are quite
one hundred and fifty species. One of the most
familiar birds belonging to this division is the robin
(*Merula migratoria*), who is quite a different bird
from his thrush cousins, how greatly different we
readily see upon making a general comparison. He
is *not* a woodland bird.

The robin's voice is pitched low, those of all the

thrushes are pitched high. The robin delights in the
close-clipped lawn, the thrush prefers the forest
tree ; he rarely comes within a hundred yards of a
house, but the robin often socially greets us quite
near the piazza steps. The true thrush is a woodland
bird ; the robin delights in the open country, and he
is companionable, but the thrush is timid and retir-
ing, and his plumage is colored so nearly like the
gray limbs of the tree, or the dead leaves below them
where he is always flitting, that we can scarcely see
him twenty feet away. But on the green lawn the
rusty breast and the slate-black crest of the robin
are prominent bits of color which are visible far
away.

The robin's warble is so very well known to us
that it seems unnecessary to take any note of it here ;
but for the sake of a little interesting comparison
with other bird music, I give two bits of his cheery
song which I think will sound familiar :

His notes are generally delivered *staccato* and in
couplets or triplets, but frequently he gives us a few
with caressing modulations, and still others slurred,
thus :

Compare this with the music of the hermit thrush further on, and it will be seen what a great difference there is in the construction of the two songs. The hermit thrush gives us no warbling note, but distinct silvery whistles in rapid triplets. It would be impossible, too, for the robin to sustain a long high note, and then " go to pieces " in silvery fragments on the next higher one, just as the hermit does. No; robin rarely ventures beyond his low-pitch, agitated couplets and triplets, but these he delivers with consummate skill.

The robin's nest is a rude, mud-plastered affair saddled on a low bough or set upon a secluded bit of ground; in it one may see from four to six most beautiful " robin's-egg blue " eggs. I use the popular color term because it is the only one which is unique, and is fittingly given. The color is a sober, delicate, yet pronounced green-blue, the like of which is not easily found elsewhere in Nature.

How much the young robin can eat is a subject for an essay; in fact, it is one which for many years past ornithologists have delighted in. But I will only repeat one marvelous and truthful account of the bird's feeding propensity. Prof. Treadwell says that from fifty to one hundred robins will eat a million worms and caterpillars in a season, and that a young one will eat in twelve hours a hundred and forty per cent of its own weight, and devour fourteen feet of earthworms! Now, if this wonderful eater would only concentrate his powers on the dreadful gypsy moth, what a blessing it would be to our elm trees! But robin eats other things as well, among which are barberries, berries of the *Phytolacca decandra*, those of the poison ivy, wild black cherries, and black alder berries. He also relishes cutworms, a fact which I recently discovered to my infinite satisfaction. The interesting way the robin carries himself on the lawn must be noticeable to the most casual observer. He stands erect and motionless for two seconds or so, then darts forward at a rapid run, and pounces upon a bit of turf in which he plunges his bill in an agitated kind of a way ; up he bobs again serenely with, maybe, a fat angleworm hanging out of his mouth, then *da capo!* If we disturb him he utters a " quirp-yip-yip-yip-yap " and flies to a neighboring tree.

A not very distant relative of the robin, but a woodland singer nearer related to the catbird, is the brown thrush or thrasher (*Harporhyncus rufus*). He is nearly if not quite twelve inches long (sometimes longer), is light reddish brown above and dull white beneath, and his breast is streaky spotted with brown ; on the wings beneath the shoulders are two white bars. The bird is a splendid singer, although his wild and irregular notes are by no means as silvery and sweet as those of his thrush cousins. He appears early in the spring, and there are those who interpret his snatchy bits of song as advice to the farmer to " plow it " or " hoe it." But it must not be supposed that his song is always so fragmentary. I listened not long since to a brown thrush, and he continued his song without intermission for ten seconds—a good long time for a bird to sing. The quality of his note is not unlike that of the robin, but he does not warble like the robin, nor does he whistle with flutelike clearness like the wood thrush ; his music is his own, and is quite as spasmodic and unconventional as it could well be.

The brown thrush frequents the thickets and copses not far from the road, and in these the rude nests are built at no great distance from the ground. There are usually five bluish eggs spotted plentifully with brown. I have found the brown thrush to be a frequent visitor of the highways which pass through the southern valleys of the White Mountains.

Where the road enters the wild wood, just under some frowning hill, there we may most likely hear, and possibly we may be fortunate enough to see, one of the greatest songsters of our country, if not the greatest woodland singer in the world. I refer to the hermit thrush, whose song once heard can never be forgotten. It is a song which we will hear from over the treetops, if the air is still at sunset, a whole mile away.

But I must first speak of the hermit's better-known relative. The wood thrush (*Turdus musteli-nus*) is rather a plain, tawny brown bird with a prominent white breast, strikingly spotted with pointed umber-brown spots, a broad, flat head, prominent eyes, and a somewhat long bill. The brown is deepest on the head and assumes an olive tone toward the wings and tail. The bill is black-brown and the feet yellow brown. The characteristic, strongly spotted breast of this bird is sufficient for its identification. The other thrushes are not nearly so well marked, and it is well to bear in mind the differences

The Wood Thrush.

which I shall point out in their breast coloring. There are four species which we ought to know apart: the wood, the hermit, Wilson's and Swainson's thrush.

The wood thrush is the largest as well as the best-marked bird of the four; as for his music, in my own private opinion it is inferior to that of the hermit thrush. But I dislike to make a descending comparison, I ought rather to say that the hermit's song is a perfected form of the wood thrush's song. Although the wood thrush delivers every note with the utmost precision of pitch (a thing which birds usually do *not* do), his tones are softer and less crystal-clear than those of the hermit. The latter also frequently indulges in a brilliant " cadenza " * (if I may be allowed the use of the term), something which is never present in the wood thrush's song. Further on I have illustrated the nature of the cadenza, upon which we may wisely depend for the identification of the hermit's song.

The wood thrush sings as late as the first of July,† morning and evening. He is not particular about sticking to triplets; often he indulges in groups

---

* A cadenza is the embellished ending of a tune; it usually begins with a well-accented high note and subsides to the key-note.

† Sometimes much later in the hills of New Hampshire.

12

of two and five notes of almost equal value. Here
are some of his (to me at least) most familiar strains:

One part of a strain which Mr. Cheney has recorded is very familiar :

His range is apparently not so great as that of the
hermit, but he has no limitation as to key. I believe
I have recorded as many as four, which I was sure
came from one bird's little throat. The best of these
two thrushs' songs is this : they can be perfectly represented by musical signs, as every note is distinctly
whistled. But we must not forget this—the whistle has no equal in all the earth, for it is born of
heaven!

The wood thrush lays her eggs (perhaps four or
five, as blue as a robin's but smaller) in a rough nest
built of grass, leaves, and mud, in a low tree or in
the bushes near the ground.

MOUNT LAFAYETTE,
FRANCONIA NOTCH,
GRAFTON CO., N. H.

THE HERMIT THRUSH.

A greater, at least a more brilliant, singer of our Northern woods, but one, however, who does not object occasionally to singing in a tree beside the highway near the pasture bars, is the hermit thrush (*Turdus Aonalaschkæ Pallasii*). This plainly attired little creature is about two thirds as large as the wood thrush. His back is an olive-brown which grows slightly ruddy toward the tail; his breast is dull white spotted with pointed spots of umber-brown, not as prominent nor as large as those of the wood thrush; immediately under the bill the throat is not spotted. His head is also broad and the eyes are prominent. The tail of the female bird is most likely to be a rufous brown. She lays three or four green-blue eggs, rarely if ever spotted, in a rude nest usually hidden under the bushes and grass on the ground. In the South the hermit thrush lives the year around, and is most frequently seen in the desolate cane swamps, flitting in the dim light which is characteristic of these regions. In the North the home of the hermit is among the mountain woods; he is always heard in early summer in the vicinity of Mounts Lafayette and Kinsman, N. H., singing along with Swainson's thrush in the half-lit spruce woods late in the day. Indeed, the hermit thrush seems to prefer a dim if not a "religious" light, which may in a measure account for the hymnlike quality of its singing, which Mr. Burroughs refers to in Wake, Robin.

But I shall endeavor to give a more tangible account of this bird's extraordinary voice. His notes are silvery, flute whistles, generally delivered in triplets. His range is quite an octave or more, and frequently he rises from a particular note to the octave higher, with surprising precision and all the eclat of an accomplished musician. I am not alone in my observation of these facts, as Mr. Cheney describes the hermit's song thus: "After striking his first low, long, and firm note, he bounds upward by thirds, fourths, and fifths, and sometimes a whole octave, gurgling out his triplets with every upward movement"—which is exactly true. How remarkably pronounced these thirds and fifths are may be seen by the following:

 (This passage is usually succeeded by that marked "cadenza.") But this is not all the hermit can do; his gymnastic exercises in the high treble are astonishing. All at once he starts with a deliberate, prolonged high note, springs suddenly to the next whole note

higher, and then falls in scintillant music a full octave, thus :

a regular tumble-down-dick cadenza, which always
reminds me of this passage near the close of Beethoven's Moonlight Sonata :

and which, by the way, is exactly repeated in Cho-
pin's Impromptu Fantasia. A more perfect bit of
bird music (except its wide range) it would be difficult to imagine.

The third songster, whose music can not possibly
be confused with that of either of the two thrushes I
have described, is Wilson's thrush, or the tawny
thrush, sometimes called veery (*Turdus fuscescens*).
This bird is a trifle larger than the hermit, and has
quite a tawny buff-brown color, the tone of which is
red, not at all like that of the wood thrush. There
are extremely few small spots on the breast, and

these begin well below the eye and extend only over the frontlet or chest; beneath, the color is dull whitish buff-gray.

The tawny thrush lays from three to five blue-green eggs in a rude nest which she builds in a low bush or on the ground; rarely the nest may be found in a low tree.

Mr. Minot says of this bird that it is rare in northern New England, but its song is a familiar one to me throughout the Pemigewasset Valley, N. H., and even as far North as Franconia. The bird is easily identified both by its color and its song. A marked characteristic of this species is a total absence of the darker color which is noticed in the tail, wings, and crest of the other species. Wilson's thrush, in other words, has a pretty nearly "all over" rufous color.

Wilson's Thrush.

One generally hears this bird singing in the gloaming, down in the lower part of the valley, generally near a brook or river. The notes are *complex*, somewhat resembling those of a reed or a violin; they are singularly double-toned and sweet beyond description, not at all like those of *any other bird I have ever heard.* When I say double-toned, I mean that the musical sound is in a certain sense harmonic* rather than melodic.

To render this song in so many *positive* musical signs seems to me an impossibility. To record a number of distinct whistles is an easy matter, but Wilson's thrush does not whistle. The notes are slurred and blended beyond the power of a musician to analyze. My rendering of the general effect would be thus : †

But sometimes there is a *pianissimo* fifth cluster of notes, dropping perhaps a musical third below the fourth cluster I have given.‡ The first and fourth clusters are exactly alike ; and to show that I am

---

* The musical note of the tree toad is double-toned, and in this respect slightly resembles that of Wilson's thrush. So, also, is that of the night hawk.

† So difficult is it to decide upon some likeness of the veery's music which may be produced at the piano, that I am tempted to suggest the discordant alternative of striking the first four notes of each cluster simultaneously ; it is at least possible in this way to more truthfully represent the mixed quality of this thrush's notes.

‡ Not infrequently the thrush begins with the second cluster and adds one more cluster at the close of my rendering of the song.

not mistaken here, I will give also the testimony of
Mr. Cheney, who renders the song thus :

He also sustains my theory of the quality of the
notes, as he says they are " something like the sweep
of an accordion through the air." This exactly ex-
presses the peculiar harmonic crescendo and diminuendo of the weird notes.

There is another thrush whose song I am not
quite so well acquainted with, but one which may
frequently be heard singing in the lonely red spruce
forests of the White Mountain region in late spring
or early summer ; this is called Swainson's thrush, or
the olive-backed thrush (*Turdus ustulatus Swain-
sonii*). I believe this bird sings only at nesting time ;
the hermit thrush sings all summer. But in June I
have often heard both birds singing at the same time.
Nothing is more subtile and charming to one's sense
of musical harmony than this exquisite, wild, silvery
music of the Northern woods. It is hardly possible
for one to pass over the highways at the feet of the
great wooded mountains of northern New York,
Vermont, and New Hampshire without hearing (at
least in May or June), *every one* of these thrushes

THE INDIAN PASS,
ADIRONDACK MOUNTAINS,
ESSEX CO., N. Y.

SWAINSON'S THRUSH.

sing.* I am quite sure of having heard Swainson's thrush in the vicinity of Lake Placid, and in the Indian Pass, in the Adirondacks, as well as among the mountains of Sandwich, N. H.

Swainson's thrush is light brown in color, tinged over the throat, breast, sides of neck and head with yellow. The general tone is not reddish like that of Wilson's thrush, but a warm light brown with a strong olive cast on the back and wings. The nest is built on or near the ground, and the eggs are green-blue, freely speckled with madder-brown.

The song of this bird is not, it seems to me, so easily distinguished from that of the wood thrush, but it is more deliberate and less scintillant than that of the hermit. Perhaps the most familiar theme is

this :

But frequently his song is made up of one long and two short notes which I can scarcely distinguish, except by their quality, from those of the wood thrush.

---

* I can at least promise the wood thrush's song in central Vermont and New Hampshire.

But before we leave the woodland road and the thrushes, I wish to call attention to another bird who incessantly warbles a few short notes among the foliage of the twilight forest iu midsummer. Just where the light takes on a shimmering green color, where the forest grows silent and solemn and stately, there is always in summer time a little bird away up in the high- est branches, per- petually sing- ing a disjointed song. This is called the red- eyed vireo (*Vireo olivaceus*). He is about six inches long, olive - backed, slaty- crowned with a dark line over the eye, and white-breasted. The hang- ing nest is usually built well up from the ground on a forked branch, and in

Red-eyed Vireo.

it one may see from three to four pearly white, madder-brown spotted eggs.

I do not see how it is possible for one to mistake this bird's song for any other. No other bird sings so disjointedly and continuously. I must except the yellow-throated vireo (*Vireo flavifrons*), however. This bird is olive-green, with a yellow throat. His song is pitched lower, and the *tempo* is less agitated. The best time to hear this music is in the afternoon of a warm day in July or August, immediately after

a shower; then if the vireo is anywhere around he
will be sure to sing. Listen, this is his refrain, in
well-marked common time:

The groups of six notes are given in a querulous
manner but with rollicking zest.

There is still another woodland bird—at least one
which may certainly be heard singing somewhere
near the top of a wooded hill, just beyond the
raspberry patch which we are passing; the voice
sounds miles away, but it is an unmistakably familiar
and characteristic one. The white-throated
sparrow—for this is the bird—is best
known by the name Peabody bird
(*Zonotrichia albicollis*). In
Wilson's estimation, this is
the largest as well as the
handsomest of all
the sparrows. His
crown is black, his
back red-brown

Peabody Bird.

umber - streaked,
and his wing feathers are light-brown edged. The
throat and breast are dull white, and over the eye
there are two white stripes. This sparrow nests in

the trees of the woodlands, and lays four or five white eggs marked with umber-brown.

The Peabody bird's song, which has a certain agreeable pathos, is remarkable for its high pitch, clear piccolo quality of tone, and freedom from the faintest trace of shrillness. It ought to be familiar to all of us who pass along the wooded road in early July. It usually comes from the top of some neighboring hill thus :

Old Sam Pea-bo-dy Pea-bo-dy Pea-bo-dy.

Frequently, however, I have heard a shorter and extremely high, soft whistle thus : *

and again the bird once in a while subsides to a more persuasive and plaintive call :

Old Sam Peabody Peabody Peabody.

* The Peabody bird sings in several keys. I have heard this particular song in two keys, in one of which the four upper notes were almost beyond the range of my whistle. As I place the limit of that at the third B flat above middle C it will at once become apparent how surprisingly high this bird can sing.

But the Peabody bird rarely sings later than July; he will be heard as late as this in the vicinity of Mount Washington, whose wooded slopes are his favorite haunts (see the frontispiece), and the following notes frequently disturb the stillness of Tuckerman's Ravine:

The best time to hear the song is early in the morning. On the whole, this is the better time to hear *all* the bird songs, and who rises with the sun in late May or early June will be favored by a full orchestra, the different members of which are distinctly recognizable. Only detached bits of the chorus can be heard at sunset, and the character of the music is certainly not so joyous.

CHAPTER XI.

RICH in emerald-green foliage and cobalt-blue skies, decked with the dainty pink of countless wild roses, and attuned with the songs of many birds, the month of June is the most beautiful one of all the year. To one who can not enjoy the brilliant green which adorns the roadside the aspect of Nature is crude and lacks æsthetic interest. But what a pity not to know that a large part of Nature's beauty is this very *force of color* after which the impressionist strives! A picturesque green roadside in New England or Illinois is quite as available a subject for an impressionist's picture as any roadside in France. We may learn to tolerate Nature in her verdant robes, but we are ready to quarrel with the artist who in copying her uses such vivid, chalky greens. I think I can show, however, that the roadside is painted with as brilliant colors as those contained in

the paint box.   Let us examine a few which are near
at hand.

One of the most beautiful bright light greens
which we will see in the swamp beside the road is
that of the Indian poke (*Veratrum viride*),* with its
spreading, broad, corrugated leaves.   Their green is
a hundred tones lighter than that of any tree, and
ten times purer.   All the beauty of color which
characterizes this plant in late May or early June
will be seen *now* ; in midsummer it sends up an uninteresting spike of green flowers, and shortly after
blackens and dies.

Another beautiful plant which is sure to decorate
the river's brink this month is the unfortunate carrion flower (*Smilax herbacea*), a charmingly decorative vine doomed to complete disfavor because of the
blossom's putrid odor.   The leaves are bright, shiny
light green, and the yellow-green flowers, now in
bloom, have very long stems ; they are inconspicuous
but pretty.   If, somewhere on the road, we imagine
we are passing a dead rat and at the same time spy a
beautiful vine-covered thicket, we are justified in
arriving at but one conclusion—carrion flower !   The
vine I have found very common in northern New
Jersey and in the southwestern region of the Cats-

---

* Its roots yield a rank poison.

kill Mountains, near Dean's Corners, N. Y. But it is common throughout the Northeastern States.

As the road climbs the slope from the meadows and enters the border of the woods, we may happen to see a pretty crimson magenta flower snuggled beside some small deep-green leaves, slightly resembling those of the wintergreen. This is the flowering wintergreen (*Polygala paucifolia*), a dainty little thing scarcely four inches above the ground, which bears its fertile flower in budlike form on a subterranean stem. The leafage is frequently suffused with ruddy purple. Still another woodland flower, and one which is endowed with the daintiest perfume, is the twin flower (*Linnæa borealis*), whose creeping stems spread over the stony ground in mossy woods, where the sunlight spots the ground with yellow-green. The little drooping bell, scarcely a third of an inch in diameter, is white lined with crimson-pink. The light-green leaves are small, round-toothed, and broadly oval. The twin flower blooms after the flowering wintergreen ; the latter is in its prime in late May.

Two noxious plants which show their bright-green leaves and greenish white flowers in June, are the poison sumach (*Rhus venenata*) and the poison ivy (*Rhus toxicodendron*). Both of these are harmful to touch, especially when in bloom. I have drawn the leaves of the plants so that they may be easily identified. *R. venenata* grows from six to eighteen feet high and bears a compound leaf composed of from seven to thirteen leaflets, smooth and without teeth. The flowers are borne in loose panicles which grow out at the junction of the leaf stem with the branch. *R. toxicodendron* is a vine which covers the stone wall and frequently climbs to the top of a small tree. Its leaves are always borne in *threes*, never in fives like those of the Virginia creeper. The leaflets are variable in shape, sometimes notched or cut-lobed, but with

Poison Sumach.

no fine teeth. They are light green with a waxy finish, and droop considerably about the stems. The flowers are similar to those of *R. venenata*; the latter species is most frequently encountered in swamps, but the poison ivy is common on every roadside in New England. Both species bear clusters of whitish lead-colored berries about the size of very small peas; they ripen in September. An excellent remedy for poisoning resulting from the accidental

13

touching of these plants is the binding of the affect-
ed parts in cloths saturated with "Pond's extract"
(*Hamamelis*). A severe case should
be referred to a physician at once.
R. venenata I have never found
in the Pemigewasset Valley, but *R.
toxicodendron* is on all of the
meadows and many of the
roadsides there.

Leaving these wretched, harmful
plants, we may now turn our attention to their near neighbor, the
handsome, spreading dogbane (*Apo-
cynum androsæmifolium*), which is just beginning to
unfold its delicate pink - white flower bells. This
thin and delicate plant gives us a refreshing bit of
sober blue-green in wide contrast with its surroundings. Its leaves are not glossy, but characterized by
what a painter would call a "dead finish." The
beautiful flowers, similar in shape to lily of the valleys or twin flowers, are daintily tinged with pink;
if we pick a cluster, the stem exudes a sticky, milk-
white juice. This plant will not reach its prime
until July, and then we may hunt through its leaves
for the most beautiful little beetle which ever favored the roadside with its presence. This jewel of
a creature is called the dogbane beetle (*Chrysochus*

Poison Ivy.

auratus). He is one of the commonest insects of
the roadside, but he is so very small (less than half
an inch long) that we must not expect to catch sight
of him at "long range." Holding one in the hand
and scrutinizing him under the glass, we will find
him a variety of brilliant me-
tallic hues, according to
the way the light strikes
his back, ranging from
orange through red to
purple, and from violet
through blue and peacock-
blue to green. I col-
lected as many as a
dozen of these beetles
last summer from as
many dogbane bushes;
their beauty and jew-
el-like brilliancy can

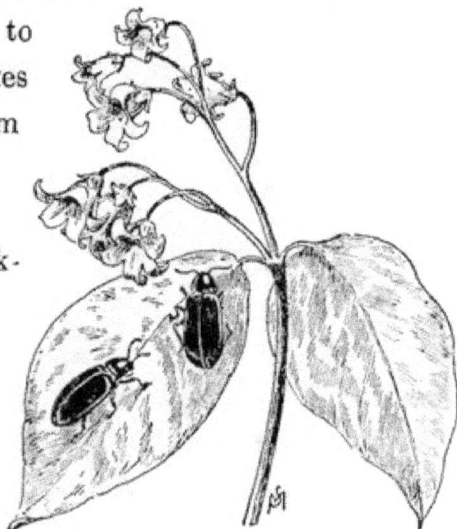

Dogbane Beetle.

only be appreciated by the help of a low-power mi-
croscope. A good test of the incomparable *finish* of
Nature's work is to place beside the beetle a ring set
with a ruby. I think the comparison will demonstrate the immeasurable superiority of Nature over
man in the capacity of an "art worker."

The roadside in the month of June is thickly embroidered with still other lusterless but ornamental

leaves. We can not proceed a dozen feet along the highway without passing at least two species of clover. The red clover (*Trifolium pratense*) is that commonest of all kinds, which bears on the face of the leaflet the looplike band of whitish green. It is largely dependent upon the pollen-dusty bumblebee for fertilization ; the crimson-red florets have such deep tubes that only the bumblebee with her long tongue succeeds in reaching the nectar in their depths.* The honeybee is only partially success-ful ; her tongue is too short, and she never attacks a blossom with the burly vigor and dauntless purpose of the bumblebee. The other common species is the white clover (*Trifolium repens*), none other than the shamrock of Ireland. I have before me as I write a cluster of the tiny leaves which but recently came from the Emerald Isle ; they are quite like our own white clover, but smaller. We can hardly claim an American origin for this species, as Gray says it is indigenous only in the Northern part of our range if at all. As for the red clover, that also came to us from Europe. The white clover, which is extremely abundant along the grassy borders of the roads in

* The first red clover which was imported into Australia failed to produce seed ; the flowers were entirely dependent upon the bumblebee for fertilization, so the insect had to be imported also for this especial purpose.

Vermont and central New Hampshire, rarely grows over four inches high. The sweetest smelling clover I know of is that called alsike clover (*Trifolium hybridum*), which strongly resembles the white kind, and which is rapidly becoming a familiar object on our highways. It has taller and more erect stems, the flower heads are larger, tinged with flesh pink and rose pink, and it does not take root as the other clovers do at that part of the stem where the leaves branch out. This species also comes from Europe.

In the latter part of June the opening blossoms of the little yellow hop clover (*Trifolium agrarium*) begin to spot the grassy borders with their delicate color. This rather upright plant would scarcely be taken for a *clover*, as its trifoliate leaf is the only strongly marked family characteristic. The tiny, pale-yellow blossoms are scarcely larger than one's thumb nail, and the leaflets are nearly stemless. Hop clover grows from six to twelve inches high and is generally found on the sandy roadside.

One other species is also just beginning to flower; this is the yellow melilot or sweet clover (*Melilotus officinalis*), whose leaves become sweet-scented in drying. It may be distinguished from the foregoing species by the blunt-toothed leaflets growing from pronounced stems. The plant grows from one to two and sometimes four feet high; it is common in waste places. The two yellow clovers also come to us from Europe. Very probably we will see at no great distance from these plants the purple blossoms of the self-heal (*Brunella vulgaris*), an omnipresent little weed which decorates the roadside from June to October. We can not fail to recognize it during the summer, as it is the only low-growing, common purple wild flower which is in bloom for fully four months of the year.

Adorning the stone wall and crowning the crowded thicket in some moist spot beside the river brink in late June, we will be sure to see the delicate pinkish flowers and arrowhead-shaped leaves of the hedge bindweed (*Convolvulus sepium*). This remarkable vine twines and trails its wiry stems over everything within reach, and ties up all the fag ends and frayed edges of the roadside foliage in

Golden Beetle.

spiral bunches of green and pink beauty. The flowers are so much like morning-glories that we can not fail to recognize them, and the fresh green leaves are among the most beautiful and shining ones of June. Somewhat later, in July, we may have the good luck to find on this vine a little opalescent, golden beetle, called the *Cassida aurichalcea*, or

Coptocycla bicolor; it is scarcely over a quarter of
an inch long, and is usually hidden on the under
part of the leaf. But once with the beautiful beetle
in our hand and under the magic magnifying glass,
we realize that we have captured a tiny gem of Nature which has no equal in the jeweler's window on
Broadway. His shell is resplendent gold, but in a
few moments it has become milky and appears more
like a yellowish opal; then it changes to a greenish
yellowish white, and finally, when we
look at it again, it is pale rusty
gold. But this remarkable
gem of a beetle is beau-
tiful only in life; when
he dies his color van-
ishes.

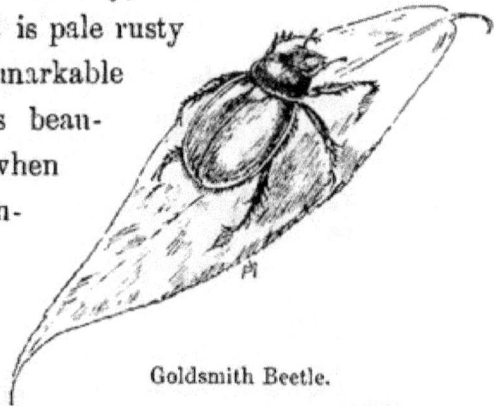

Another splen-
did and common
golden bug is the

Goldsmith Beetle.

goldsmith beetle (*Cotalpa lanigera*), which still
later in the season we may succeed in capturing on
the under side of a willow leaf; he is about seven
eighths of an inch long. This beetle is abroad at
night and sometimes ventures in an open door, lured
by the brilliant lamplight within; but in daytime
he hides himself completely among the clusters of
fresh green leaves at the tips of young branchlets.

His back is bright yellowish gold, sometimes of a milky tone ; beneath he is copper-color, covered with fine whitish hairs.

In a partially shaded spot beside the covered bridge which crosses the shallow mountain stream we may be favored by the sight of many golden flower clusters of the wild parsnip (*Pastinaca sativa*), or those of its near relative, the early meadow parsnip (*Zizia aurea*). In some damp spot near the river—on the meadow perhaps—these tall weeds are sure to appear in June. Their favorite attendant is the black, yellow-spotted butterfly (*Papilio asterias*),* sometimes called the "black swallowtail." This is one of the commonest and prettiest butterflies which visit the roadside flowers. Its wings are marked with a double row of yellow spots ; there are also yellow and bluish marks on the hind wings as well, and these are *swallow-tail pointed*. This butterfly invariably chooses some member of the Parsley family, on the leaves of which it prefers to lay its eggs. The caterpillar is pea-green, naked, and about two inches long.

The monarch, or tawny orange butterfly (*Anosia plexippus*),† which is also commonly seen on the

---

* *Papilio polyxenes,* Scudder.

† Also called *Danais archippus* and *Danais erippus.* Its powers of flight exceed those of any other butterfly. It migrates

SHELVING ROCK, MADISON,
JEFFERSON CO., INDIANA.

THE BLACK SWALLOW-TAILED
BUTTERFLY.

highway, whose beautiful wings, measuring four inches across, are bound and veined with black, white-spotted, has a decided preference for members of the milkweed tribe, but not infrequently we find it hovering over the dainty pink blossoms of the dogbane (also a milky juiced plant). However, the common milkweed (*Asclepias Cornuti*) is its favored plant, and on the upright budding leaves it lays its eggs singly. The caterpillar of this butterfly is black and yellow banded, naked, and nearly two inches long. How handsome this

Anosia plexippus.

very ordinary milkweed is in sunny June, when its pale-green color is dashed with misty lilac-blue shadows, and its æsthetic brown-lavender flower cluster is accented by the rich coloring on the wings of the monarch butterfly, no one can fail to remark. It is one of those few striking plants which are emphatically decorative under all conditions and in all seasons.

Fluttering over the little puddles on the road

in autumn and flies southward in swarms as the birds do. The body of this butterfly has a rank odor.

which are left after the rain, a half dozen small yellow butterflies appear, dispersing as we approach, but soon returning to continue their dance in midair as soon as our backs are turned; these are the *Colias Philodice*,* which in the caterpillar state live on the leaves of the clovers. The caterpillar is an inch long and grass-green; we will generally see it stretched along the stem of a clover leaf. I have drawn the yellow butterfly beside the pretty vista which it might have seen if it had not devoted itself so exclusively to the uninteresting puddle in the middle of the road. The view is of one of the southern Catskill Mountains, called Big Indian, not very far from Shandaken.

The little white butterfly which we may occasionally see is called the cabbage butterfly (*Pieris rapæ*).† This is the plague of the farmer, for its green caterpillar bores to the heart of his cabbages. The eggs are laid on the under side of the leaves and hatched in about ten days; the caterpillars then feed upon the young green leaves for about twenty days, at the ex-

Pieris rapæ.

---

* *Eurymus Philodice.* Scudder.
† First introduced into this country in New York, 1868.

BIG INDIAN, CATSKILL
MOUNTAINS.
ULSTER CO., N.Y.

YELLOW BUTTERFLY,
COLIAS PHILODICE.

piration of which time they have gorged sufficient raw cabbage to attain a length of one and a half inches. Then they leave the garden and resort to the rocks or the fence, and spin thereon a tuft of silk in which they place their hind feet; a loop is then spun in which they hang by the neck. After eleven or twelve days have elapsed the green worm has become a white butterfly, ready to begin on the cabbage patch again! I never see a white butterfly without a picture arising in my mind of a certain indignant farmer, who never missed an opportunity of flapping at one with his old gray

Papilio turnus.

felt hat, which the butterfly always managed to evade.

One of our largest and most beautiful butterflies is the pale corn-yellow and rusty black one (the upper parts of the wings are marked with four descending black bars), with swallow-tailed wings, called the tiger swallowtail (*Papilio turnus*).* This handsome creature frequently measures four and a half

---

* *Jasoniades glaucus*, Scudder.

inches from one wing tip to the other. It soars even above the trees and takes to the broad expanse of sky as the yellowbird does. The caterpillar lives in the orchard and feeds upon the leaves of the fruit trees, or resorts to the birch, poplar, and ash. It is two inches long, fat and green, with rows of bluish dots and black and yellow markings, and the head and feet are pink-tinged. Early in August this caterpillar tires of life and "hangs" itself in a leaf cradle bound together by silken cords; the following summer it resumes life in the form of a gorgeous velvety winged butterfly. I often see the handsome creature perched on top of the pasture thistle, but according to the rules of entomology I believe it has no right to be there. Yet I understand that the thistle is favored by many broad-winged visitors, chief among which is our yellow friend *Colias Philodice*.

Those tiny little butterflies, which flit about with an uncertain motion, but a short distance, from one blossom to another, are called "skippers" (*Hesperia*). They are generally marked and spotted red-brown and yellow, and proceed from small caterpillars which wind themselves up in leaves drawn together by silken threads. The skipper butterfly will scarcely measure an inch across with wings extended; it also frequents the pasture thistle. A very common spe-

cies is *Hesperia Pocahontas* (*Atrytone zabulon*, Scudder), sometimes called the Mormon. Its wings are
blackish brown, marked in the center with tawny
orange-brown. It is very abundant in early June,
and feeds and nests among the roadside grasses.

The leafy month of June is glorious in the absolute purity and diversity of its greens. Look at that
shining white-stemmed tree yonder ; it is the gray
birch, whose pea-green, varnished leaves flash the sunlight through the intervening branches of the brown
and rugged pine, until the sparkling color dazzles the
eyes. At the farther side of the road is a thicket
of speckled alder ; its color is deep somber olive.
Look at the tips of the red maple near by, and note
the pinkish green of the yet immature leaves. Here
is a baby red oak ; its large leaf is deep olive-
green, its budding leaf is bright red. Yonder is a
white poplar ; how remarkable is its flickering, pale
color !

If we are fortunate enough to see the splendid
yellowwood (*Cladrastis tinctoria*) in full bloom
toward the end of the month, we will think that
it is one of the most beautiful trees of June. No
apple tree of May in snowiest array can equal it,
for there is little of grace in the gnarled apple, and
naught but grace in the yellowwood. So rich is
it in nectar, too, that all the insects from the sur-

rounding country congregate in a busy, buzzing, fluttering swarm to gather the fragrant sweet.

Another beautiful tree is the yellow chestnut oak (*Quercus Muhlenbergii*), whose yellowish green leaves reflect an amber light and cast misty lilac-blue shadows. These are the brilliant colors which the impressionist sees and endeavors to portray on his canvas. It is one thing to paint a well-composed landscape, but it is quite another to paint the vivid sunlight and the emerald foliage of June. What wonder then that the painting which the artist brings directly from sunlit Nature dazzles our eyes! It is a fact that we are too timid to look Nature square in the face when she is decked in her liveliest colors; we are afraid of them, and are in no mood to dance to such lively piping. We like brilliant colors best in tiny bits like those of the green, yellow-spotted beetle (*Buprestis fasciata*) which I have drawn below; his gorgeous emerald back often decorates the roadside fence, and it is exempt from criticism.

Buprestis fasciata.

CHAPTER XII.

In the warm days of August most of the singing
amid the treetops has ceased, and life has taken on
a different aspect for both bird and man. Every
winged dweller in wood and meadow finds food
in plenty, with never a hungry bill to fill beyond
his own. We listen to the grasshoppers' summer
symphony and count it a signal for relaxation, an
audible proof of the fact that the time has come
when it is too hot to do anything but keep quiet.
Nature, however, does not idle, nor does she slacken
her energy in time of heat; the borders of the highway are the best evidence of this fact. At no time
of the year are the hedges and thickets so crowded
with luxuriant and rank vegetation, nor have we
seen until now such an aggregation of tall, striking
weeds. The margin of the highway in May was flat
and empty compared with its present aspect. Now,
on the edge of the meadow and at the side of the

191

road, a midsummer family has taken up its quarters, most of whose members are sufficiently tall to look over the fence. Many of them measure three and four feet, and several six and even twelve feet in height. These magnificent weeds are nearly all members of the great Composite family, the records of which occupy a large section of Gray's Manual.

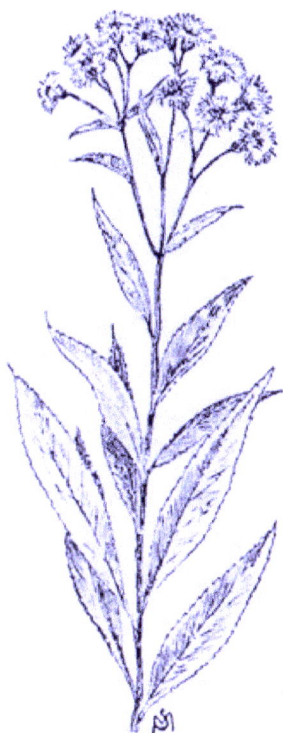

The first familiar flower which Gray mentions is the ironweed (*Vernonia Noveboracensis*); this is common near the seashore. It grows from three to five feet high, and its clusters of purplish magenta flowers, from which the bees gather quite a little honey, somewhat resemble tiny sweet sultans or bachelor's buttons; but it is a rude, stocky, useless weed, with a stout, hard stem which cumbers the ground. It blooms in August. Next come the *Eupatoriums*, a coarse tribe not without some saving, useful qualities. Boneset (*Eupatorium perfoliatum*)

Ironweed.

is perhaps the best-known member of this group, and we can always tell it by the way the stem seems to perforate the opposite - growing leaves which taper to a point. The flowers are dull white, small, and uninteresting. The plant grows from two to four feet high and has a coarse hairy stem. It is a bitter herb, whose medicinal properties we are well acquainted with, but one whose flowers we would never suspect the bee finds stored with honey.; such is the case, however.

Joe-Pye weed (*Eupatorium purpureum*) is another tall relation with dull

Boneset.

pinkish flowers. The leaves are very rough and veiny, and the simple, stout stem grows from two to twelve feet high. This is rather an aspiring weed, which furnishes the lowland landscape in summer with the most consummately æsthetic pink tone which it is possible to imagine. A good patch of Joe-Pye weed under a hazy August sky produces one of those delicious bits of cool pink, set in dull sage-green, such as an impressionist likes to paint. The

14

commonest weed by the roadside becomes one of the most beautiful things in the world when the strength of its color is portrayed on the impressionist's canvas. We may look at it skeptically, but the artist reveals a real not an imagined beauty, which all of us have eyes to see quite as well as he.

If the general color effect of Joe-Pye weed is attractive, the delicate beauty of white snakeroot (*Eupatorium ageratoides*) is greater. This beautiful weed grows beside nearly every woodland road in the North. The flowers are dainty copies of the soft, woolly blossoms of the ageratum in our gardens; the leaves are ovate-pointed, long-stemmed, and coarse-toothed. The whole character of the plant is smooth, not hairy, and its slenderer stems grow from three to four feet high. It is one of the refined members of the *Eupatorium* family group.

White Snakeroot.

Passing the multitudinous golden-rods and asters, to the most important of which I have devoted a chapter further on, we come to two of the commonest shorter weeds of the roadside : these are robin's plantain (*Erigeron bellidifolius*) and daisy fleabane (*Erigeron strigosus*). The former looks like a blue aster out of season ; it blooms in May and June along moist banks and shaded byways. The latter appears like a miniature aster, either perfectly white or slightly tinged purple ; it blooms from early June to late September. Both of these plants grow, at most, not over twenty inches high. The sweet scabious (*Erigeron annuus*), however, is a plant with a more imposing presence. It is a tall weed, usually three and sometimes five feet high, with a stout, much-branched stem beset with little hairs, and narrow upper, but broader lower (coarsely toothed) leaves. The white or purplish flowers have short rays and broad, dull-yellow centers. This is a very common weed in the waste places beside the road, and one which I often find in company with the coarse burdock.

Next among our tall weeds (but these are not so very tall) are the familiar white everlastings. Pearly everlasting (*Anaphalis margaritacea*) is quite the handsomest species. It grows from one to two feet high, and the stem is leafy to the top which expands in a large, broad head of white flowers. The best way to distinguish this species from the common ones is to examine the little petals (really *scales* of the involucre) under the magnifying glass ; if these are white, obtuse, and rounded, radiating with age, the flower is that of the pearly species ; if they are ovate and oblong but still obtuse, the flower is one of the species *Gnaphalium polycephalum* ; if they are yellowish white, oval, and pointed, the flower is that of *G. decurrens*. Other differences between the three species, all of which are common on our roadsides which pass the hillside pastures, are these : *G. polycephalum* grows from one to three feet high and is fragrant ; its leaves are lance-shaped with narrowed base and wavy margins, the upper surface free from wooliness. *G. decurrens* grows about two feet high, and its narrower leaves partly clasp and extend down the stem ; they are cottony on both sides. The leaves of *A. margaritacea* are long, lance-shaped, quite green above, and they clasp the stem.

Elecampane.   Another familiar wayside weed, one of those tramps long since arrived from Europe but still " on the road," is elecampane (*Inula*

THE LOWLANDS.

JOE-PYE WEED.

Helenium). This is a tall, stout herb, with stems from three to five feet high, whose mucilaginous roots have been used as a horse medicine. The flowers are yellow with extremely narrow rays and coarse yellow disks; the leaves are large and woolly beneath, the upper ones clasping the stem slightly, and the lower ones distinctly stemmed. Elecampane is usually found on damp ground where the road passes the swamp, in which thousands of grasshoppers and crickets swell the grand chorus of a midsummer day's song. The drowsy music is not easily separated in my mind from a weedy wilderness of burdock, golden-rod, and elecampane; for that matter we do not have to peer beyond the topmost leaves of the latter plant to see a musician or two; undoubtedly, if we look sharp, we will behold a grasshopper (more properly speaking, a locust) sitting contentedly on his high perch, a listener if not a performer. His name is *Melanoplus bivittatus*, and he with his red-legged cousin, *Melanoplus femur-rubum*, the commonest of our field locusts or grasshoppers, finds the succulent leaf of the *Inula* furnishes a very delectable luncheon in the middle of a hot day. These two insects are always perched on the big, dusty leaves of the roadside. I have never seen either of them alight and sit still; they always turn at least a quarter of the way around, and thus make sure of covering the four points of the compass in as many acrobatic leaps.

We now come to the tallest member of the Composite family, the ragweed (*Ambrosia trifida*), which grows from four to twelve and occasionally eighteen feet high. This extraordinary plant is commonly found in waste places. Its tall, straight stem with large, deeply three-lobed leaves and terminal stalks of greenish flowers is one of the most striking things of the highway border. In the fall, if a dried dead stalk is broken, we will find it contains an unsubstantial white pith with a sheen like frostwork. The tall and slender but stout-stemmed ragweed when growing in damp, rich soil, often shoots beyond the twelve-foot mark. I have found one specimen which measured over thirteen feet, and William Hamilton Gibson records one that measured eighteen feet four inches.

Black-eyed Susan (*Rudbekia hirta*) is the next flower which engages our attention ; its deep golden, orange-yel-

The Ragweed.

low rays and its purple-brown "cone" are familiar
to us all. But few of the flowers are left by midsummer—they were in their prime in early July.
It is not a tall plant—rarely a few stems stand two
feet high. Our common garden sunflower (*Helianthus annuus*) is a near relative of *Rudbekia*. An
allied species often found on the roadsides of the
North and East is *Helianthus giganteus*, a small
flower with bright-yellow rays and a fairly good
yellow center; this prefers the shaded
nooks and corners of fields and woodlands. Not far from the sunflower,
perhaps in some moist spot near a
passing brook, we may find we have
come in contact with the troublesome
weed named beggar-ticks (*Bidens fron-
dosa*); wherever we have touched the
plant our clothing is covered with its exceedingly tenacious, two - pronged seed
vessels. The insignificant flowers are   Beggar-ticks.
rayless, and rusty yellow in tone, and
the leaves have from three to five divisions. This
uncomfortable roadside weed is from two to six feet
high; it blooms from June to October.

Also in the wet ground there is every chance of
finding (at least as far North as Pennsylvania and
Connecticut) the budding stems of the tall sneeze-

weed (*Helenium autumnale*), which may be from one to six feet high. The flowers, about half an inch broad, are yellow-rayed and have duller yellow disks; sometimes the brighter rays droop. The leaves are lance-shaped and toothed. This weed blooms in September.

Along our roadsides in the East is a common European weed whose white-rayed flowers closely resemble daisies; this is the May-weed or chamomile (*Anthemis Cotu-la*). Its finely cut leaves and small flower heads, with yellow centers in

Sneezeweed.

high relief, are sufficient means for its recognition; but, by bruising the leaves the strong familiar odor of chamomile proves the identity of the low-growing plant beyond a doubt. The common daisy (*Chrysanthemum Leucanthemum*) we may find still in bloom beside the chamomile.

Golden ragwort or squawweed (*Senecio aureus*) is common in the lowlands, and blooms as early as May or June. It grows from one to three feet high, has a very variable leaf, and bears pretty golden-yellow flowers which look like small, deep yellow daisies. It is one of the first members of the Composite family to bloom, and we will hardly find a flower left by the first of August.

If we should happen to pass a wooded clearing which has been burned over, here we will see the coarse, heavy, grooved stems of the fire-weed (*Erechtites hieracifolia*), with its alternate, lance - shaped, · cut - toothed leaves waving in the passing breeze. The stem grows from one to five feet high and terminates in an ample panicle of small white flowers somewhat tubular in shape. It is a rank-smelling (often hairy stemmed) weed of unattractive appearance. But quite its equal in disagreeable odor is the common burdock (*Arctium Lappa*), which one invariably finds in the waste ground beside some old, abandoned farmhouse. Every one knows how tenacious the little hooked

Fireweed.

tips of the burs are; children frame baskets with the clinging things, and those who visit the deserted house on the neglected byway, usually carry away numerous burry souvenirs of the occasion on their clothing. But burdock has an æsthetic if not a homely interest, for the artist finds it an indispen-

sable and picturesque accompaniment of the "old farmhouse" which is the theme of his picture.

The Canada thistle (*Cnicus arvensis*) is another dweller in the highway and the pasture which came to us from Europe. Gray calls it "a vile pest in fields and meadows." The flower heads are not more than an inch long and very numerous; the tips are lilac-magenta.

The common thistle (*Cnicus lanceolatus*), with the large and handsome flower, is also naturalized from Europe. The base of the deeply cut leaf runs down the stem in prickly wings; the flowers are also lilac-magenta. Our tallest thistle (*C. altissimus*) is common in copses and on the borders of the road and field from Massachusetts to Minnesota and Southward. Its stem, from three to ten feet high, is leafy quite to the flower head, which is purple or rarely white, and from one and a half to two inches long. The leaves are very woolly beneath, wavy, and the topmost ones are not very deeply cut. This species is indigenous. On sandy roads near the coast, from Massachusetts to Virginia, is a yellow thistle (*C. horridulus*), with a stout stem one to three feet high, partly clasping, smooth, green, yellow-prickled leaves and flower heads, about two inches long and an inch and a half broad, yellow, or rarely purple-topped, and surrounded at the base by a circle of prickly leaflets (bracts). This species is also indigenous. In early September we will probably see the little yellowbird picking at the ripened thistles in the pasture; he is after the seed, and if we watch him we will see how nicely he aids Nature by setting whole clouds of thistle down afloat.

The most perfect of all blue wild flowers now follows in our list: it is *par excellence* the roadside beauty. This is chicory (*Cicorium Intybus*), a dandelionlike flower whose charming misty blue set in soft green must be seen in broad spreading masses to be appreciated. The flower is too familiar to need description here. Its roots are ground, roasted, and used either to flavor coffee or to furnish a straight substitute for it.

Still another dandelionlike flower we will see on the rattlesnake weed (*Hieracium venosum*). This scrawny stemmed plant grows from one to two feet high, and bears on its many branches small yellow flower heads composed of strap-shaped florets. The leaves, clustered at the root, conspicuously purple-veined above and purple-tinged beneath, are oblong, thin, pale, and slightly, if at all, toothed.

A hawkweed (*Hieracium Canadense*) which is quite common on the woodland roads in the North bears yellow flowers slightly resembling the species described above. It has a simple leafy stem growing from one to three feet high, bearing at the top a somewhat flat flower cluster. The leaves are lance-shaped or oblong, acute, and sparingly coarse-toothed; the uppermost leaves slightly clasp the stem. I have found this flower in bloom in northern New Hampshire in August. *Hieracium scabrum* is a roughish, hairy stemmed species with a stout, simple stalk two to three feet high, having reversed egg-shaped or oval leaves without teeth, and a narrow cluster of many small flower heads which are thickly clothed with dark, glandular bristles. This is a very common species of dry, open woods, and it frequently appears on the shady roadside.

Hieracium Canadense.

We now come to the last section of importance in the Composite family, the tall *Prenanthes*. The commonest member of this group, lion's foot or gall of the earth (*Prenanthes serpentaria*), we are quite sure to meet in some shady stretch of the highway. This weed bears pretty, drooping, bell-shaped flowers, variously colored with green, dull purple, and dull yellow-white. The leaves are somewhat angularly shaped ; the lower ones are variously three- to seven-lobed, with mar-gined stems ; the upper ones are oblong, lance - shaped, mostly undivided, and they almost clasp the main stem. This plant will also be found in the tangled brush of the clearing, where its inconspicuous flowers are scarcely relieved against a confused and green background; it blooms in late August.

The tall rattlesnake root (*Prenanthes altissima*) is an imposing species common in the rich woodlands of the North, which sometimes attains a height of seven feet. It bears a long narrow panicle of inconspicuous green and dull-white flowers, which top off the slender weed with a slightly curved,

Prenanthes serpentaria.

loose, leafy cluster, and also spring from the junction of the leaves with the main stem. The leaves are variously shaped, but all have distinct stems ; they are triangular, ovate, toothed or cleft, and frequently three-to five-parted. Still another species, *P. alba*, sometimes called common white lettuce, is also quite frequently found on the woodland road in the North; this grows from two to four feet high and bears inconspicuous white or greenish florets, enveloped in purplish scales. The leaves are also very variable.

These three species of *Prenanthes* are characterized by *drooping* flowers.

Another species common throughout the extreme North is *P. racemosa*; this bears purplish flowers which are nearly erect. The stem rises from two to five feet in height, and bears oblong, lance-shaped leaves, toothed, smooth, the upper ones slightly clasping the main stem, and the lower ones tapering into margined stems next to the main stalk.

The tall rattlesnake root has but one rival of imposing stature; that is the marvelous ragweed. Whenever we see a slender climbing stalk beside the road, it is pretty sure to be one of these two giant weeds, which spend the greater part of spring and summer in an effort to reach the sky.

Prenanthes
altissima.

THE FRANCONIA NOTCH,
FROM CAMPTON, GRAFTON CO., N. H.

CHAPTER XIII.

THE BEES WHICH WE PASS BY.

THE common honeybee (*Apis mellifica*)* is an omnipresent little creature which is always in search of honey and pollen among the roadside flowers. What is most interesting about this insect is its family history, which I will take it for granted every one knows. The marvelous economy of the beehive we have long since become familiar with through the writings of Agassiz and Langstroth ; † and as for Langstroth, we ought to be proud to know that the world is indebted to him, an American, for enlarging the science of bee culture and inventing the *one* perfect and ingenious hive in universal use to-day.

In late June, when the patches of raspberry brambles are in full bloom beside the road which leads

---

* The Italian bee (*Apis Ligustica*) is quite as common.

† Lorenzo Lorraine Langstroth was born in Philadelphia, December 25, 1810.

northward through Campton to the Franconia Notch, we will be sure to find the Italian honeybee busily engaged there. It is always the worker bee, never any other, and we can only call her a female in a limited sense of the term, as the queen or mother bee is the *one* perfectly developed female in the hive; *she* only lays the eggs.* The worker, we can easily see by a glass, is busy dipping her long, triple-shaped tongue in the nectar. This she draws up by the trough-shaped middle division of the tongue, and it is conducted into the honey-sac (the equivalent of a stomach); on the way it undergoes a chemical change from cane sugar to grape sugar. This is accomplished by the admixture of a salivary secretion of the bee with the flower nectar. The bee's stomach is furnished with muscles which enable her to compress it and thus ejaculate the honey into the comb cell. We will see, therefore, that honey by the time it reaches the hive is no longer simple flower nectar any more than a raw oxhide is shoe leather.

But honey is not the only thing which the bee gathers, and Watts did not record in his familiar verses the other important part of her work; she

---

* Very rarely, however, when a colony has been queenless for some time, a few workers are sufficiently developed to be capable of laying eggs; but these eggs only produce drones. (Langstroth.)

very often collects pollen. This she carries in certain
bristle-edged hollows in the sides of her hind legs,
called pollen baskets. I rarely find a bee on one of
my garden flowers with her baskets empty; she
usually has them crammed full to overflowing with
the golden dust. Dust it looks like to
our dull eyes, but under the micro-
scope it takes on the loveliest forms,
several of which I have sketched.
However, the bee does not gather it
for æsthetic reasons; she wants it for
food, not only for herself but particularly for storage in the cells of the
bee mother's brood. If both honey
and pollen can be gathered from the
same blossom, the industrious bee will
not leave until she has collected a good
load of each. Wherever she begins

The Worker Bee
and magnified
Pollen.

there she will stay, no matter if the pollen is not
quite as plentiful as it is in some other flower; consequently, the contents of the baskets are nearly always one color, either yellow, orange, or brown. In
fact, the bee does not care for "mixed fruit," and
it has been explained that the mixed kinds do not
pack so well together. When the load of pollen is
brought home it is brushed out of the baskets into
the cell, packed down very carefully, covered per-

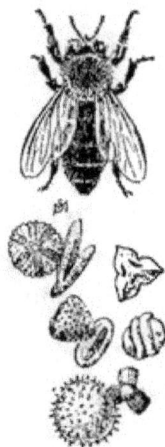

15

haps with honey, and the cell is sealed over with wax ready for future use.

Very early in the morning, when my ranunculus poppies are in full bloom, they are alive with thousands of bees intent upon gathering pollen. The musical hum of their wings can be heard thirty feet away, and so intent are they upon the pleasant task, that occasionally I can stroke a fuzzy, pollen-besmeared back with my finger tip and meet with no sign of remonstrance. The bumblebee, however,

The Italian Bee.

objects; but she, too, is altogether pre-occupied, and she only demurs by kicking up her hind legs. Nearly all the bees which visit my garden are Italians. They are distinguished from the common bees by the five golden bands on their abdomen, the middle one of which should be distinctly visible; the other four are less pronounced, especially if the little creature is *not* stuffed full of honey. This Italian bee (*Apis Ligustica*) was introduced into this country in 1859 by Messrs. Wagner and Colvin, of Baltimore, and its superiority in every way to the common bee is conceded by all apiarists. It is less sensitive to cold, more peaceable, less apt to sting, more industrious, fights better against the enemies of the hive, and is more easily handled than the common bee; the latter is slate-gray in color and varies greatly in size, but is generally a trifle plumper than the Italian bee.

The common black bee was introduced into Florida by the Spaniards some few years previous to 1763. Longfellow evidently knew that the honeybee was not indigenous to this country, for he makes Hiawatha say of the white men :

> Wheresoe'er they move, before them
> Swarms the stinging fly, the Ahmo,
> Swarms the bee, the honey-maker.

One of the most interesting facts about the work of the bee is the method she pursues in the manufacture of wax; this is evolved by a sort of meditative process somewhat akin to German philosophy, except that I must admit the irrelevancy of mind in this particularly ease. The workers proceed to gorge themselves with honey ; then they hang together in a series of chains from the roof of the hive, each one clasping hands with her neighbor and remaining in that quiescent position for twenty-four hours or so. This inactivity produces a result similar to that which follows upon the cooping up and overfeeding of a barnyard fowl ; the bees begin to grow fat—that is, they exude wax in the shape of delicate scales from eight small pouches on the under side of the abdomen. Honey is therefore converted into wax in much the same way that food is converted into fat. But these wax scales are so tiny that four hundred of them would scarcely outweigh a kernel of corn; and as for the quantity of honey which the bees must consume to promote this interesting operation, *that* seems incredible, for it has been estimated that no less than from seven to ten pounds of it are required for the making of one pound of wax. What an expensive process!

The remarkably beautiful queen or mother bee is a veritable aristocrat. Notice how different her figure is from that of the plebeian worker or the drone. Her wings are proportionally short and as fine as gauze; her body is long and tapering, and underneath it is golden yellow. She is rarely, if ever, seen away from the hive, and then, perhaps, only when the bees are swarming. Nearly all of her life is spent indoors, and her time is quite absorbed in heavy maternal cares. In the laying of eggs the barnyard hen is not to be mentioned in the same breath with her, as in breeding time she can lay at the rate of three hundred and sixty eggs per minute, and sometimes she produces not less than thirty-five hundred in one day! If she made as

A, the Drone; B, the Queen Bee.

much fuss about it as an ordinary hen, what an interminable racket would greet our ears from the beehive!

The flowers and trees which line the side of the road offer stores of honey for the bee; let me mention some of them, for they are by no means the strong-scented ones. The raspberry (it bears the finest flavored honey) stands at the head of the list, next comes white clover. Red clover is hardly eligible because the bee's tongue is not long enough to reach down to the bottom of the blossom; so we must leave this flower to the bumblebee whose tongue is longer. Then comes the dandelion, rich in both pollen and honey, and the wild rose, melilot, Canada thistle, all fruit trees, red and sugar maples, linden, all willows (these furnish both pollen and honey), Judas tree, yellowwood, locust, tulip tree (one of the greatest honey-producing trees in the world), hawthorn, snapdragon, larkspur, borage, chamomile, mignonette, alyssum, coreopsis, sunflower, boneset, ironweed, fireweed, rudbekia, thoroughwort, catnip, horsemint, dead nettle, basil, peas, beans, false indigo, chicory, golden-rod, aster, and, last but not least, that characteristic roadside flower, self-heal (*Brunella vulgaris*), a blue-violet flower which is the especial favorite of the bumblebee. I should not omit to include the common milkweed, but this is a great snare for the honeybee.

The milkweed flower's pollen is gathered in a compact mass inclosed by a tiny sack. These sacks are connected together by threads which terminate in a single sticky gland ; this adheres to the feet and the outer parts * of the poor bee's tongue, and she soon is so ensnarled with threads and pollen bags that she falls to the ground and perishes. The bee can, however, clean herself off if she is not too much encumbered, and under the magnifying glass it is quite amusing to watch her " tidy up." She uses her saliva for water, cleans off her feet and legs, combs her antennæ with her fore legs, which are especially constructed for the purpose, smoothes down her wings by brushes attached to her heels, even brushes her eyes instead of wiping them, and when she has completed her toilet flies away with an evident feeling that she is now " fit to be seen." She does not fly slowly either, for she can champion the fleetest bicyclist and the most famous race horse by a record of more than a mile in two minutes.

The bee's life is rather short, not over thirty-five or forty days long in the busy season of summer. In winter, however, a period of comparative idleness, it is estimated to extend over a much greater length of

---

* The labial palpi and maxilla, accessory parts of the tongue proper.

time; but with the exception of the queen, no bee lives to be a year old.

The bumblebee or humblebee (*Bombus*)* is even more commonly a searcher after honey on the roadside than the honeybee. It is scarcely possible to see a patch of red clover, or a little clump of the pretty blue *Brunella vulgaris* at our feet, without some one of the blossoms holding a golden-hipped, smoky-winged, clumsy visitor, one of the very best of flower friends because the most useful pollen disseminator in the world. The humblebee is so called because it builds its nest on the ground beside the grasses, or under stones. The colonies of bumblebees are small compared with those of the honeybees; sometimes there are as many as three hundred in a

The Queen Bumblebee (*Bombus Pennsylvanicum*).

family, but frequently not more than fifty or sixty. In each nest there are four kinds of bees—the queens, small females, males, and workers. In autumn all except the queens die; these remain dormant in the deep seclusion of some hole near the nest until the warmth of returning spring awakens them from their winter lethargy, and prompts them

---

* There are about forty different species.

to look about for some suitable spot in which to lay their eggs. The situation being duly selected, the bee goes a-foraging for honey and pollen ; these she works together in a mass and on it deposits her eggs. Very soon the eggs are hatched, and the grubs after eating and growing fat finally envelop themselves in silken cocoons ; then the mother bee covers the cocoons with wax. Eventually the young bees mature and emerge from their cells, full-fledged workers. This *modus operandi* is repeated until several broods are hatched, the small females and the males being produced about the middle of sum-

The Bumblebee
(*Bombus vagans*).

mer, and still later the queens from the *final* batch of eggs.

The bumblebee is a little glutton, either on the roadside clover * or the garden sunflower. I have watched more than one cram itself so full of honey from my sunflowers that apparently it was helplessly drunk with the potent sweet. The thistle seems to produce the same effect on the greedy insect, and, despite all urgent invitations to move on, it either clings to the flower or drops to the ground with a hopeless, maudlin kind of a buzz !

There are insect characters often seen among the

---

* See also Chap. XI, page 180.

roadside flowers which so closely resembles in appearance the golden bumblebee that I must draw attention to the points which distinguish them apart.

One is called *Eristalis flavipes*. It is a near relative of the drone fly and a harmless sipper of honey. The other is called the robber fly, and its Latin name is *Laphria*, or *Dasyllis tergissa*. This bloodthirsty individual hangs about the flowers of my garden, or carries itself with innocent mein on the roadside goldenrod, as though it was bent on honey; but let a small insect approach too

The Robber Fly.

near and the murderous hypocrite will pounce upon it, thrust a horny bill in its side, and draw every drop of blood from its body. We can always identify him by two or three unmistakable characteristics: he has only *two* wings, not four like the bumblebee or any other bee; then his shoulders are *dull*-gold color and are not *humped* like those of the bumblebee; besides, there is the formidable horny bill which, under a glass, bears no resemblance whatever to the bumblebee's honey tongue. Still another robber fly (*Promachus bastardi*), of a wasplike figure, is frequently seen among the roadside flowers.

Eristalis
flavipes.

One word, now, about bees' stings. As for the bumblebee, she is good-natured beyond measure, and the honeybee very rarely stings. Of course, all male bees and wasps *have no stings*, so they can be handled with impunity. A little calmness in the presence of numberless bees will go a great way toward preventing a painful misunderstanding; but to thrash the air with one's hat is to invite hostility. It is often said that if the honeybee stings once, she seals her own fate and must inevitably perish. This is not so; it altogether depends upon circumstances. The tip of her sting is not like that of a hornet, smooth and needlelike; it is barbed with a number of very tiny points set laterally, so that when she stings deeply—we will say about a fourteenth of an inch down—these catch on the flesh like the teeth of a saw, and the enraged insect, tearing herself away, or, more likely, thrust violently aside

The Robber Fly
(*Promachus bastardi*).

by her victim, leaves not only her sting, but her poison bag and other portions of her anatomy behind her. Under such conditions she can not continue to live. But should she sting less deeply, or strike the tender, soft flesh of a less muscular individual, she will probably escape uninjured. Should it happen

that the bee's sting enters the flesh perpendicularly, it is more likely to be safely withdrawn; but if it enters at an angle, as it usually does if the bee bends its abdomen forward, then the sting is left behind. In this event it should be instantly removed by a rapid scrape to the right or left with the nail or the point of a penknife. To withdraw the sting by pulling with the two fingers is to incur the possible risk of pinching the poison bag and injecting more poison into the wound.

CHAPTER XIV.

THERE is no better place to study the colors of
Nature than on the highway. Here we may obtain
the best effect of light on mountain and intervale,
and the greatest color depth in the shadows of bordering trees; here the sunshine on the birches looks
greener than it does elsewhere, except in the woods,
and the emerald of the mountain pool ceases to be
fancy, but fact. The neutral gray-buff of the road
furnishes an admirable canvas, so to speak, on which
the colors, as in a picture, reveal their *true* strength
and beauty.

I have elsewhere spoken of tone deafness; it is a
fact that some ears lack either the ability or the
training to hear properly. In the same sense there
are many of us who do not properly see color in
Nature. Years ago, when the impressionists first ex-
hibited their work in Paris, they were ridiculed by

WILLOWS BESIDE THE ROAD.
THORNTON, GRAFTON CO., N. H.

artist and critic ; now the ridicule of impressionism is confined to an unappreciative public. This means that some of us have learned that we were partially *color-blind*, and did not see all the color in Nature which the impressionists *did*, and to obtain which they let everything—perspective, drawing, modeling, and composition—go to the winds. I am strongly of the opinion, therefore, that to see color properly we should learn to see it as they did—in an *exclusive* manner.

But it is my purpose here to suggest how we can train our eyes to see as much of Nature's color as may be possible. There are countless numbers of greens in the leafage about us ; let us see how wide the differences are. A leaf of the long-beaked willow (*Salix rostrata*) is an excellent example of contrast. This willow is sure to be on the roadside, and we may know it by its thick, broad, rough, and irregularly scalloped leaf which is deep olive-green above and pale-blue white-green beneath. A slight gust of wind sets it in motion, and we catch glimpses of olive and white which are quite impressive. This whiteness is a marked feature of some willows, and after a little study it should soon be possible for us to know them a mile away by their blue-white-green color. The attenuated form of the foliage is largely accountable for this light and soft color effect ; the sunlight does not readily get at the narrow leaves, and they reflect very little light. Quite the opposite is true of a young leaf of the gray birch (*Betula populifolia*). This is bright, shiny yellow-green, very responsive to sunlight, and in strong contrast with the dull dark hue of the long-beaked willow leaf. But of all the yellow-green leaves which we can find in the woodland not one is comparable to that of either the young red mulberry (*Morus rubra*) or the young Indian poke (*Veratrum viride*); these are inexpressibly tender and pure in color.

It is only by comparison that we can gauge the strength of color. Red reveals its full power only by its environment; this can be proved in an instant by a very simple experiment. Suppose we take a bit of purple paper, and, cutting a round hole in the center, place a bit of scarlet paper behind it; next, we will treat a bit of yellow paper in the same way, placing another piece of the same scarlet paper behind that. What is the result? The two scarlets no longer appear *equally strong*; that behind the yellow paper seems to be much darker!

The distant mountain appears quite blue; but if there is a lingering uncertainty about that, it all vanishes if we will suffer for an instant the discomfort of turning our heads upside down and viewing the landscape that way. The mountain is now intensely

GRAY BIRCHES IN SUNLIGHT,
AFTER A SHOWER.

blue, and the stretch of meadow down in the valley is intensely green ; we had not noticed that before. This may be accounted for by a very simple fact : in disturbing the normal position of objects on the retina, we disturb also our acute perception of detail. As there is little or no detail to color, we see that *en masse* without visual distraction : and when our attention is exclusively devoted to one thing we are apt to understand it better—that is all. As a matter of fact, the eye becomes dull and heedless from seeing things in the ordinary way, and a little shaking up acts as a positive stimulant.

The omnipresence of color in Nature is not fully appreciated ; occasionally, by accident, we discover more color than we think we have any right to see! It is precisely in this conservative spirit that we criticise an impressionist's uncommonly colored picture ; we think that he can not truly see so much, and has wilfully made his picture a chromatic falsity. But we ourselves have not learned the whole truth about color until we have turned our heads upside down !

Nature uses no black in any part of her work— I will not even except the blackberry * and the so-called black pansy. On a bright, clear day, the

---

* See the chapter containing a description of the blackberry.

shadows on the snow are pale ultramarine blue; under a blue sky in midsummer, the color of the placid lake is cobalt blue and the shadows on the grass are lilac; on a weathered, gray board walk they are nearly as blue as the sky itself. The palpitating atmosphere of a warm July day lifts the coloring of the landscape to a higher but softer key instead of reducing it with gray; and in autumn, when the sugar maple's leaves are turned to gold, the shadows on the trunk, and every gray rock in the vicinity, are tinged with *strong* lilac. In fine, when the sun shines, everything, even the shadow which we are prone to believe is gray, is replete with color.

Not even the neutral buff-gray of the road is exempt from blue-tinted shadows; look at them through a small hole in a bit of white paper and the blue will become more apparent; where does it come from? I can answer the question best by suggesting two experiments which demonstrate the peculiar effect of colored light; they are both simple and conclusive. If we light two small lamps in a dark room, one with a red and the other with a blue-green glass shade, place them about two feet apart, and eight feet away from some small object within nine inches of the wall, we will see on the latter two shadows, one of which is green and the other red.

Now, if we turn down the red light the green shadow disappears, or if we turn down the green light the red shadow disappears. So we discover the fact that while the two lights are turned up each throws its color in the shadow produced by the other. Again, if we light a white-shaded lamp in the daytime (it should be a cloudless day), and place it on a table covered with a white cloth in a room where the light is admitted through but one window, the shadow of a napkin ring on the cloth cast by the lamplight will appear quite blue. In this instance we have discovered that the daylight, more or less influenced by the reflected blue of the sky, casts a blue light in the shadow thrown by the lamplight.

Now our blue shadows out of doors are thoroughly accounted for; the intense blue sky *throws a blue light in every shadow* cast by the sun. It is also the fact that the purple of distant mountains is partially due to the blue of the sky above. The poet Whittier more than once has alluded to "the purple of mountain sunsets." The word purple, however, but vaguely describes the roseate hues cast upon the blue mountain by the setting sun. If we will turn our head upside down again and study the sunset glow on the far-away hills, we will see there nearly every color related to purple, but hardly purple itself; the summits of the rocky hills are bathed in a

16

rosy glow, this is reduced to crushed-raspberry color as it fades away on the wooded slopes beneath, and down in the deep ravines is a whitish, violet-ultramarine shadow too soft to suggest in the remotest way the crudeness of true purple.

In broad daylight the flower-decked meadows covered with tall, ripe grass are seldom green; instead, we have buff, yellow, yellow-green, salmon-pink, whitish pink, and shadowy lilac again. In early June the golden-green patches of buttercups resemble the colors on the humming bird's back. In later June masses of ox-eye daisies throw a dainty pinkish white tint over the grass, and in July the wild Canada lily embroiders it with a powdered pattern in tawny yellow. But I never see any brown or gray on the meadow; it is always brimful of color, from the glare of light on the white daisies to the lilac shadows of the tall, graceful elms. Even in winter, when it is covered with a mantle of snow, it is still rich in color, for its borders are set with the almost vivid red stems of the red osier (*Cornus stolonifera*), its pure white is accented by the iridescent blue-black of half a dozen stray crows; and best of all, just before the sun sets (however freezingly cold the effect may be), the white is tinged with yellow, and the broad shadow of the opposite hill which is creeping over it is intensely purple—exactly the

IN STRONG SUNLIGHT.   A ROAD IN ILLINOIS.   AFTERNOON.

Crows on the Frozen Meadow.

color that Whittier thought he saw in the mountain sunset. But chilly yellow and purple are sunlight and shadow colors which belong to winter, never to summer; we always find them in frosty skies and on frozen meadows. Undoubtedly there are gray days and leaden skies in plenty, even in midsum-

A gray day.   Road to Blue Island, Ill.

mer, but these only serve to accent the rainbow tints of sunshiny days, and to rivet our attention particularly on those wonderful transient effects of color which occasionally favoring us at the sunset hour, prompt us to exclaim with some vehemence: "There! if an artist should put *that* color effect on canvas, every one would say he did not tell the truth!"

CHAPTER XV.

GOLDEN-ROD AND ASTERS.

GOLDEN-ROD is a distinctively American flower, not only indigenous to our country, but broadly distributed from one end of it to the other. There are in all no less than seventy-five members of the tribe *Solidago* (Composite family), forty-two of which are described in Gray's Manual of Botany. But there are only a dozen or so species which are common on the borders of the highway.

The golden-rods have two distinct kinds of leaves. I have drawn these, and they tell their own story at

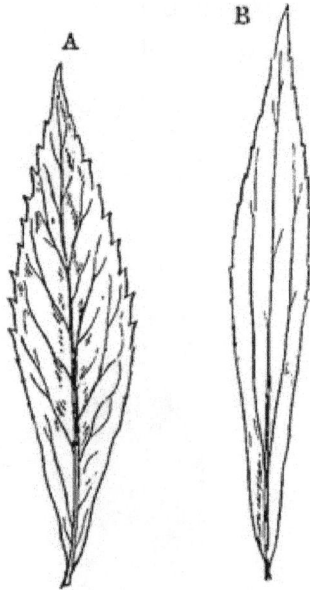

A, Feather-veined Leaf;
B, Three-ribbed Leaf.

229

a glance. We will call one a feather-veined leaf and the other a three-ribbed leaf. All the golden-rods, therefore, can be divided into two groups distinguished apart by the kind of leaf. Beyond this leaf difference there are other distinguishing characteristics of the plants which are to be referred to the flowers and the plant stems; these are not difficult to discover.* The questions which naturally arise as we pursue our investigations are these :

1. Is the leaf smooth or rough-hairy ?

2. Is it plain-edged, or toothed, or both—i. e., " half and half " ?

3. Is the stem of the plant straight or angled ?

4. Is it woolly or smooth, or covered with a plum-like bloom ?

5. Is it cylindrical or angular if cut in a cross section ?

6. How many little petals (rays) are there on one floret ?

7. Do the flowers grow in feathery plumes, or in flat-topped clusters, or in little bunches along the stem ?

Each golden-rod common on the roadside I will describe after the order suggested by these questions.

---

* A magnifying glass is an almost indispensable aid in the solution of these little botanical problems.

1. *Solidago arguta.* Blooms about the middle of July. Leaves feather-veined, but not very distinctly so, large, broad, smooth, the lower ones sharply toothed, the upper ones without teeth ; in shape, oval, sharp - pointed at both ends. Stem angled, smooth, angular in section, and sometimes ruddy brown. Flower, *light* golden yellow, fully a quarter of an inch long, with six or seven large rays. Flower plume long and gracefully curved. If the plant is one-stemmed and small the flowers will spring from the junction of each leaf with the stem. This species is common in copses and the borders of woods ; it grows from two to four feet high.

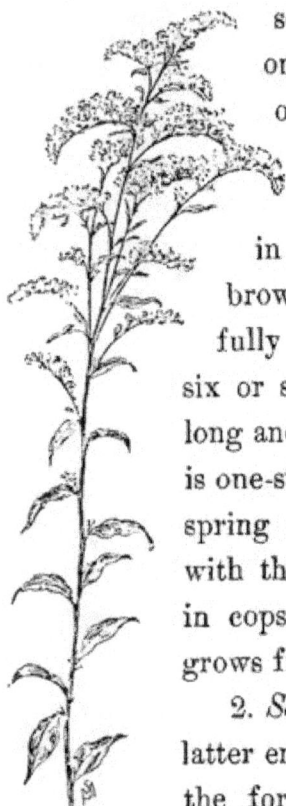

S. arguta.

2. *Solidago juncea.* Blooms about the latter end of July ; often in company with the foregoing species. Leaves slightly three-ribbed, smooth ; lower ones large, somewhat elliptical, sharply toothed, the teeth spreading ; a tiny leaf wing grows out on either side of the leafstem where it joins the stem of the plant ; upper leaves generally without teeth, shaped like willow leaves. Stem straight and smooth, not perfectly cylindrical in section. Flower small, golden yellow,

one sixth of an inch long, with eight to twelve small rays. Flower clusters spread symmetrically like the

S. juncea.

S. serotina.

figure of an elm. The smaller plants have *one-sided* clusters. This species is common on roadside banks and copses; it grows about thirty inches high.

3. *Solidago serotina*. Blooms about the first of August. An upright, dignified species often found in company with *S. juncea*. Leaves plainly three-ribbed,

smooth, and toothed only along the *upper half* of the edge; they are narrow and sharp-pointed. Stem stout, smooth, perfectly straight, cylindrical, and very often covered with a plumlike bloom, but sometimes light green. The stems of the little flower clusters are covered with the tiniest of white hairs. Flower small, light golden yellow, with seven to fourteen long rays. Flower clusters spread cylindrically at the top of an unbranched stem. A taller species than the preceding, rarely reaching a height of six feet, common beside fences and in copses. Not found at the seaside.

4. *Solidago nemoralis.* Gray golden-rod; the Latin name means belonging to the woods. Blooms about the tenth of August. Leaves three-ribbed, covered with minute grayish hairs, broad lance-shaped, dull-toothed, somewhat wider at one end than the other; the lower ones taper very narrowly toward the stem. The stem is gray, covered with tiny grayish hairs, and is always simple, never branched. Flower *deep* golden yellow, with five to nine rays. Flower clusters crowded together forming a one-sided plume gracefully curved. This species possesses the most brilliant color of all the golden-rods; it rarely reaches a height of over two feet, and is common beside the road and in the pastures. Its thinly leaved, single stem is, on the

average, eighteen inches high. Not found at the seaside.

5. *Solidago bicolor.* White golden-rod. Blooms about the tenth of August. Leaves feather-veined, rough-hairy, especially the veins on the under surface, only sparingly toothed, and dark olive-green above; the lower ones quite large, elliptical, and pointed at both ends; the upper ones small and lance-shaped. Stem straight, generally simple, and covered with soft grayish hairs. Flower yellow-cream color, with from five to fourteen *white* rays; in effect remotely resembling the color tone of mignonette. Flower clusters growing from the junction of the leaves with the plantstem short, and crowding into a cylindrical spike at the top of the plant. This species is not showy; it is common on dry ground.

S. bicolor.

6. *Solidago lanceolata.* Lance-leaved golden-rod. Blooms on or before the tenth of August. Leaves light green, three-ribbed, sometimes five-ribbed, without teeth, and extremely narrow willow-shaped; the edges scratchy-rough. Stem straight, angular in section (the ridges which run lengthwise with the

stem are minutely rough), and terminating in a radiating, much-branched flower cluster. Flower tiny,
in little crowded clusters, with fifteen
to twenty short rays, light golden
yellow. Flower clusters flat-topped
and not showy in color, supported by
small-leaved, wiry stems. This species
is common on river banks, in wet shaded
places, and on the borders of woods; it
grows from two to three feet high.

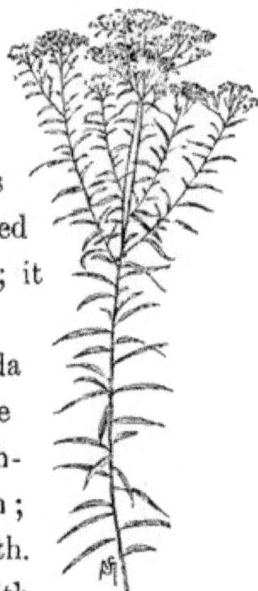

7. *Solidago Canadensis.* Canada
golden-rod. Blooms about the middle
of August. Leaves three-ribbed, rough-
hairy, sharply toothed, and deep green;
sometimes they are almost without teeth.
Beneath, they are always covered with
soft, downy hairs. Stem rough-hairy,

S. lanceolata.

stout, and hardly cylindrical. Flower small, greenish golden yellow, with from five to seven short
rays. Flower clusters spread with graceful curves
in an ample plume sometimes one-sided. A very
common species on the borders of roads, thickets,
and fields, varying greatly in the roughness and
hairiness of stem and leaf, and growing from three
to six feet high. Not found at the seaside.

8. *Solidago rugosa.* Rough-stemmed golden-
rod. Blooms about the middle of August. Leaves

feather veined, deeply toothed, very veiny, exceedingly rough and hairy, and dark green ; in form variable, from broad lance-shaped to elliptical or oblong. Stem straight, cylindrical, thickly beset with leaves, and much branched at the top. Flower light golden yellow, with from six to nine rays. Flower clusters not remarkable in color, much beset on the branchlets with little leaves, spreading, and formed of minor clusters about three inches in length. A very common species found on shady borders of the road, presenting a great variety of forms, chief among which is the cluster of leafy branchlets terminating a leafy, stocky stem ; it grows from one to six feet high.

S. rugosa.

9. *Solidago ulmifolia.* Elm - leaved golden-rod. Blooms about the middle of August. Gray says of this species, " Too near *S. rugosa* ; distinguished only by its *smooth* stem and thin, larger leaves." The upper branchlets are hairy, and the flower has about four rays. This species is common in low copses near streams which pass beneath the road ; it grows about three feet high.

10. *Solidago odora.* Sweet golden-rod. Blooms about the middle of August. Leaves bright green, indistinctly three-ribbed, smooth, or very nearly so, without teeth, shining, and somewhat dotted. Stem slender and usually smooth, often reclining, and nearly cylindrical. Flower small, with three or four large, golden-yellow rays. Flower clusters spreading in one-sided, rather small plumes. The crushed leaves of this species yield a pleasant aniselike odor. *S. odora* is common in dry and sandy soil, particularly near the coast; it frequently occurs in the pine barrens of New Jersey. It grows from two to three feet high.

11. *Solidago cæsia.* Blue-stemmed golden-rod. Blooms about the first of September. Leaves dark-green, feather-veined, smooth, distinctly toothed, lance-shaped, and pointed. Stem slender, slightly angular, covered with a plumlike purple bloom, reclining, and often much-branched. Flower very large, bright golden yellow, with from three to five large rays a full sixteenth of an inch broad. Flower clusters small and hemispherical or oblong, like those of the lilac; they are arranged along the curved stem at the points from which the leaves grow. This species, although not particularly effective, is one of the handsomest of all; it loves the shady, wooded roadside, and grows about three feet high. We

should know it at once by its bluish stem and exceptionally large, light-yellow florets.

12. *Solidago latifolia.* Broad-leaved golden-rod. A species similar to the preceding, and blooming at the same time. Leaves deep green, feather-veined, broadly oval, sharply toothed, and conspicuously pointed at both ends. Stem smooth, without the blue bloom, angled, zigzag, and generally simple, but sometimes branching at the tip. Flowers light golden yellow with but three or four rays. Flower clusters small and arranged along the stem like *S. cæsia.* This species is also common on woodland borders.

Blooming at the same time with several of the golden-rods, we will see a dozen kinds of asters purpling the roadside with a handsome array of starry blossoms. Of the forty more or less common species which we meet with East and West, there are a few which we will find both attractive and interesting. These I will describe in the same systematic manner as I have the golden-rods.

1. *Aster Novæ-Angliæ.* New England aster. Blooms in late August. Leaves very numerous, lance-shaped, sharp-pointed, without teeth, minutely hairy, and slightly clasping the stem. Stem stout and hairy. Flower pale violet (rarely magenta-purple), as large as a silver quarter, or larger; numerous,

and widely distributed over the stems. Common on moist ground. The most familiar wild aster, now extensively cultivated.

2. *Aster Novi-Belgii.* Willow-leaved blue aster. Blooms in September. Leaves narrow, lance-shaped, without teeth or with a very few, usually a trifle hairy; sometimes quite rough above, and in a few forms wholly smooth, the upper ones somewhat clasping the stems. Stem smooth or slightly hairy. Flower bluish violet, showy, as large as a silver half dollar; the little green scales underneath loose. This species is common along the Atlantic border; it blooms late, and is rarely over two feet high.

3. *Aster puniceus.* Purple-stemmed aster. Blooms about the first of September. Leaves very rough-hairy, oblong lance-shaped, very slightly narrowed at the stem-clasping base, pointed, without teeth, nearly smooth beneath, and dull green. Stem stout, rough-hairy, and *madder-purple*, particularly below. Flower lilac-purple or paler, as large as a

Aster Novi-Belgii.

silver quarter or larger, the little narrow green scales beneath sharp - pointed and loose. An extremely common but variable species found in low thickets and swamps, from three to seven feet high.

4. *Aster radula.* Rough-leaved aster. Blooms in late August. Leaves oblong lance-shaped, pointed, sharply toothed in the middle, very finely rough on both sides, and absolutely stemless. Stem smooth or slightly hairy, many-leaved. Flower pale violet, about an inch and a quarter in diameter, with short spreading green tips beneath. A common species on low grounds, usually about twenty inches high; frequently lower.

5. *Aster patens.* Spreading aster. Blooms about the middle of August. Leaves ovate oblong, or sometimes longer, rough above and on the margins, without teeth (or very rarely with small ones), and stemless. Stem rough-hairy, terminating in slender branchlets which bear the flowers. Flower purple, with spreading, pointed green tips beneath; it measures an inch and a half across. This species is common on the shaded borders of the highway, usually on dry ground; it grows from one to three feet high.

6. *Aster undulatus.* Wavy-leaved aster. Blooms about the middle of August. Upper leaves ovate lance-shaped, with wavy or slightly toothed margins,

roughish above, downy beneath, the topmost ones stem-clasping. Lower leaves without teeth, pointed, heart-shaped, with long stems which flare out widely at the base and clasp the stem of the plant. Stem grayish, covered with finest hairs. Flower lavender-purple, about an inch and an eighth in diameter. A species also common in dry shady places by the road, growing usually twenty inches high.

7. *Aster cordifolius.* Heart-leaved aster. Blooms early in September. Leaves on the lower part of the stem heart-shaped and toothed; those above narrower and much less toothed. Both leaf and stem of plant variable as to smoothness or rough-hairiness. Flower extremely small, about three quarters of an inch in diameter, lilac, and blue-lavender, crowded in dense clusters like lilacs. A common species on wooded banks, growing not over two feet high. A variety frequently found on the roadsides of the White Mountain region, bears *nearly white* flowers about five eighths of an inch in diameter, narrow leaves, and grows about eight inches high.

8. *Aster spectabilis.* Showy aster. Blooms from early September to November. Leaves oblong lance-shaped, rough, mostly without teeth, only the lower ones obscurely toothed. Stem roughish. Flower showy, bright light violet, with about twenty rays nearly an inch long. Very few flowers on the stems.

17

This species, one of the most beautiful of all, is confined to the seacoast; its range is from Massachusetts to Delaware. It grows from one to two feet high.

The most familiar species of white asters are the following:

9. *Aster paniculatus.* White, panicled aster. Blooms about the middle of August. Leaves dark green, smooth or nearly so, broad lance-shaped, sharply toothed, the upper ones less conspicuously toothed. Stem stout and much-branched. Flower white or very nearly so, about an inch in diameter, crowded in *flat clusters.* A very tall species, from three to eight feet high, common on moist, shaded banks.

Aster paniculatus.

10. *Aster umbellatus.* Tall, white aster. Blooms about the middle of August, and Southward earlier. Leaves long, lance - shaped, smooth, taper-pointed and tapering at the base, generally without teeth. Stem smooth, stout, leafy to the top. Flowers numerous, white, with but *few* rays, the short green scales beneath rather close and obtuse; the clusters are *flat-topped.* This species is

common beside moist thickets; it grows from two to seven feet high.

11. *Aster corymbosus.* Slender, white aster. Blooms very early, from July to the first of September. Leaves ovate, lower ones heart-shape based, thin, smoothish, coarsely and unevenly sharp-toothed, taper-pointed, and olive-green. Stem slender and somewhat zigzag. Flowers with from six to nine white rays borne in small loose clusters. This species is common in *woods* and beside the woodland road; it grows from one to two feet high, and is not showy.

12. *Aster ericoides.* White, heathlike aster. Blooms from the middle of August, or earlier, to late September. Leaves *tiny* and slightly hairy, narrowly lance - shaped and light green.

Aster ericoides.

The lower ones are broader at the upper end; rarely they are toothed. The stem is nearly smooth and set with spreading branches. The *tiny* white flowers resemble miniature daisies; the clusters terminate the erect branchlets. This beautiful little aster is common in dry open places of certain localities in New England. It is familiar on the roadsides of the South and West, and in many a stony field its white,

starry clusters mingle with the yellow plumes of the gray golden-rod.

The colors of the roadside in September are exactly the reverse of what they were in early June.* The asters and golden-rods are now tinting it with purple and yellow, two colors which are strikingly beautiful in combination with the greenish gray of stone walls and rocky ledges, which are rapidly coming into plainer view with the thinning of the foliage. The swampy hollow, which some time ago was lined with the white of daisies and the gold of buttercups, is now swept broadly by the sober, grayish lilac of the purple-stemmed aster; the meadow has exchanged its emerald hue for a less vivid, warm rusty-green; the white-blossomed hedge is no longer white, but yellow with the plumes of the Canada golden-rod; and the borders of the highway, once monotonously green, are now decked in a thousand tints of golden yellow, lilac, purple, lavender, pale scarlet-orange, pink, and rusty-red—a mosaic of infinite beauty on a sunny day.

---

* The prevailing colors of June are, of course, the bright green of foliage and the pink of roses.

CHAPTER XVI

EARLY in the autumn, on the shady roadside where the golden-rod grows, it is quite likely that we shall find the pretty three-leaved vine called the hog peanut (*Amphicarpæa monoica*) twisting its stems about every available tall weed. It is one of those peculiar plants which has two kinds of flowers—a pretty little lilac one in a nodding cluster which rarely ripens fruit, and a subterranean one without petals and somewhat pear-shaped, from which results a seed resembling a peanut. The leaves are very light green and without gloss. The name, which is derived from the Greek, signifies "both kinds of fruit," as the flower above ground occasionally produces a miniature pea-like pod containing three or four seeds in addition to the one beneath ground which produces the "peanut." There is still another similar vine called the groundnut or wild bean (*Apios tuberosa*), which we

will find climbing over the roadside thickets. This
is the one that Whittier's barefoot boy could find for
us as easily as a botanist; he knew better than any-
one else

> Where the groundnut trails its vine.

It bears from three to seven ovate lance-shaped
leaflets, and rich clusters of beanlike blossoms, dull
purple-brown in color, and somewhat violet-scented;
they bloom in late summer and through September.
The groundnut is quite common in low ground
through the North, from Maine to Minnesota. I
have drawn with the vine a bit of Whittier's country; a glimpse of the beautiful Merrimac River not
far from Newburyport, Mass.

Among our blue wild flowers there are none pret-
tier than the gentians which appear in the autumn
months. The fringed gentian (*Gentiana crinita*) is
the most beautiful of the species, although I do not
consider its color as striking as that of some of
the other less handsomely formed gentians. The
"fringed lids," as Bryant calls them, of this flower
constitute its essential point of beauty.

The common closed gentian (*Gentiana Andrew-
sii*) is far more interesting in color if not in character; the blue is variable and is broken by plaits of
white where the corolla is folded together. The
flower is perhaps one of the most puzzling and in-

MERRIMAC RIVER,
NEAR
NEWBURYPORT,
MASS.

GROUND NUT,
APIOS TUBEROSA.

teresting subjects of our floral world. How the blossom is fertilized, whether it depends entirely upon itself or upon insects for the proper disposition of its pollen, is a question which has never been satisfactorily answered. But a casual glance at the flower persuades us to believe that it takes care of itself. If we doubt its conservative character, let us try to force our way to the stamens and learn how difficult the task is, for the corolla must be torn to pieces to do so. Yet the bumblebee finds a way in. This persistent little plunderer will take a flower by storming the citadel if necessary! Mr. Clarence M. Weed has witnessed the struggle, and I quote what he says : " With some difficulty it thrust its tongue through the valves of the nearest blossom ; then it pushed in its head and body until only the hind legs and the tip of the abdomen were sticking out. In this position it made the circuit of the blossom and then emerged, resting a moment to brush the pollen from its head and thorax into the pollen baskets before flying to a neighboring aster." Gray has also said that he has seen the bumblebee force its way into a closed gentian, but during a number of seasons 1 have watched in vain to catch the robber in the act.

Still another beautiful blue flower we will find common in the Northwest ; this is *Gentiana puberula*, whose color is equal to the azure-violet of the sky at sundown on a cold September evening. The corolla is vase-shaped, topped by five pointed divisions. The plant is from eight to fifteen inches high, and the stem is mostly rough with tiny fine hairs at the top. The leaves are stiff and long lance-shaped. This species of gentian is common in the vicinity of Minneapolis, the Minnehaha Falls in the country of Hiawatha, and on the dry borders of the great wheatfields of Minnesota. The soapwort gentian (*Gentiana Saponaria*) is another Western species which we will occasionally see on the roadsides near damp woods from New York west to Minnesota. The light lilac-blue corolla is but slightly open, and the five blunt lobes or divisions are almost erect. The leaves are broad lance-shaped and rough-edged. The stem is smooth and about a foot or eighteen inches high.

The five-flowered gentian (*Gentiana quinqueflora*) is a slender-stemmed branching plant with broad lance-shaped leaves partly clasping the stem, and clusters of five flowers at the summit, pale lilac-blue; the corolla is funnel-formed with five bristle-tipped lobes. This flower is found on hillsides from Maine to Illinois; it grows in the vicinity of Lake Mohunk, and commonly through the Shawangunk Mountains. It is also found in the northern hills of New Jersey.

Whoever heard of a stone wall bordering the hill-

LAKE HARRIET, MINNEAPOLIS,
HENNEPIN CO., MINN.

GENTIANA PUBERULA.

side highway which passes through the North country without its chipmunk? Perhaps the zigzag rail fence may enjoy the exclusive reputation of being a distinctly American institution, but the green-gray stone wall, with its bittersweet, squirrel, and woodchuck, I consider no less a product of American soil. The like of it we will not see in the old country.

Italy is full of glaring, plastered, forbidding walls and barren, walled-in roads with never a touch of rural life or interest for passing travelers.* The country is worn out with the poverty of its inhabitants, and exhausted of every green thing that ought to grow on the wayside.

We do not appreciate our native land, with its wealth of green plants and its multitude of trees, nor do we realize the boundless life and liberty of our fields and woods and open roads. The ferns, golden-rods, asters, and gentians which grow by the wayside, the birds and squirrels which scamper over the fence rails, the woodchuck who burrows beneath the stone wall, the pretty green snake which winds sinuously among the grassy borders, the tree cricket, and the piping hyla—these all testify to an abundance of wild life which is unknown in the old country.

---

* I might add also that they lack bucolic interest, but for the fact that Italian shepherds do exist!

Our little striped squirrel or chipmunk * (*Tamias striatus*) is one of the most interesting creatures of his kind in the world. His color is chestnut-red, and down his back run three distinct, almost black bands with the two outermost marked down the middle with a line of white. The little creature is astonishingly spry and moves with a jerk or else sits upright with his hands crossed before his breast. His tail is narrow and not very long; indeed, he is altogether different from the pictures which we see in English books of the European squirrel (*Sciurus vulgaris*).

The Chipmunk.

He is passably tame, and I have no difficulty in watching him for hours together at a distance of not more than four feet as I am at work in my garden. Should I happen to be in his path he will not trouble himself to take a circuitous route, but will skip fearlessly across my toes. Of sunflower seeds he is extremely fond, and the butternuts which are

---

* This is the so-called Eastern chipmunk. The four-striped chipmunk (*T. quadrivittus*) is commonest, perhaps, in the Mississippi Valley, and is more widely distributed over the country; he has four whitish stripes upon his back inclosed within five black ones. Of course, the stripes of *T. striatus* can be counted as five black and two white, as well as the three compound stripes I have described.

so common among the old pasture lands of the southern White Mountains are his trees of plenty.

The chipmunk is a stone wall squirrel. He is a very poor tree climber, and when he meets the red squirrel on a low bough he instantly concedes to him the right of way. But on the stone wall he will chase his red cousin from Dan to Beersheba, although I have never yet found him engaged in a fight to protect his right of eminent domain. On the contrary, I have long since concluded that the chickaree or red squirrel * (*Sciurus* † *Hudsonius*), quite a little larger than the chipmunk, and of an even, burnt sienna-red color, with a black streak on his flank, is an aggressive and quarrelsome individual, disposed to attack his chipmunk cousin or one of his own species on the slightest provocation. I have seen him chase another squirrel around the trunk of a butternut, which was his castle and home, no less than twenty-five times in the space of half a minute. He has a noble fashion of vociferously claiming whole tracts of wooded country as exclusively his own—at least we may believe so if we have learned to understand his words

* His range is throughout North America as far as the forests extend.

† This name in Greek means "he who is under the shadow of his tail," which hardly applies to our short-tailed chipmunk and chickaree.

and actions. On the highway he is a bit more respectful and does not attempt to interfere with a passing wheelman, but in the woods he swears roundly at any base intruder. Somebody has likened his scolding to the winding of a clock—a not far-fetched simile; but what an outrageously asthmatic clock, and what a dreadful need of grease on the mainspring! When we enter the wood in nominal possession of the red squirrel this is about the kind of greeting we may expect: "Wretches! wretches—both, chuck which, chuck which, chuck which, chuck 'em out! quick, quick, quick! Chuck which-which-chuck-which, chuck-which, chuck which, chuck 'em both out quick, quick, quick, chuck——" and with a whistle of alarm he disappears around the other side of the tree just as a pebble has been sent within a yard of his saucy chin! The red squirrel's voice is threatening; there is no mistaking the fury of his wrath which visibly quakes his whole body to the very tip of his tail.

The large gray squirrel (*Sciurus Carolinensis*) I do not find as plentiful in Campton as the other two species; for several seasons past, very few have appeared in the wood or on the roadside. In Roxbury, a part of Boston, they are quite common among the trees on some of the old estates, and they are often seen in the hemlock grove in the Arnold arboretum.

Nothing can be more graceful than their scalloped lines of flight along a tree bough.

The gray squirrel is a sociable little animal who likes the company of a man with a few nuts in his pocket. One can not walk across the square in Richmond, Va., without encountering two or three tame individuals who regard a man as a species of animated nut tree created for his especial benefit!

If we will watch a squirrel closely we may observe him tuck away two or three small nuts in his cheeks and carry another in his teeth. Last summer one of my friendly chipmunks made six journeys within two hours from a certain corner of the house to his nest beneath a fence post by the road, for the purpose of transferring his summer stores. One would suppose upon beholding his bulgy cheeks that he was afflicted with a severe form of mumps.

The flying squirrel (*Sciuropterus volucella*) is a tiny, gray, silky-furred creature, often made a great pet of. His eyes are round and liquid, and his chubby little face is expressively intelligent. This squirrel is a most remarkable trapezist; he takes a flying leap from the top of one tree to another, and covers forty or fifty feet with ease. It is recorded that he can leap one hundred and fifty feet! He is active mostly at sundown, and sleeps during a greater part of the day. A little pet I once owned would sleep comfortably during the day in my pocket or the elbow of my sleeve, but was ready for a grand scamper in the evening.

The flying squirrel is furnished with a marvelously expansive skin which greatly aids him in his aërial exploits. He is common entirely across the continent.

Not far from the roadside, by some stream which proceeds from the woods, we may possibly see the splendid color of the bright-red flower called Oswego tea or bee balm (*Monarda didyma*). But this is generally beyond its prime by the first of September: still, we may find an occasional flower here and there. The blossoms—something like those of our garden salvia in form—are clustered at the top of the stem. This handsome wild flower is common from New England to Michigan. I have often found it on the borders of damp woods in the vicinity of Stony Clove and Shandaken, in the southern Catskills. It has a somewhat hairy, angled stem, and opposite-growing, ovate-pointed leaves emitting an aromatic odor if crushed. The smaller leaves near the flower cluster are tinged reddish. Oswego tea and its garden relative, *Salvia splendens*, which comes from Brazil, belong to the Mint family.

By the close of September we are compensated for the loss of the brighter wild flowers by the glo-

rious red, orange, yellow, and maroon of the turning leaves. The brilliant hues of autumnal foliage are produced mostly by the ac-
tion of the cold atmos-
phere on the chlorophyll
or green matter in the
microscopic leaf cell.
Chlorophyll is a marvel-
ously complex substance difficult to analyze. It is
found in solution in an oil
which fills the interstices
of what is called the chloro-
plasts (the masses of spongy substance which fill the cells beneath
the upper skin of the leaf). By
a chemical change, therefore, the
green color of a leaf is destroyed, and a red or yellow color takes its place. But the scientific fact is
less interesting to us than the æsthetic result of
the change.

Oswego Tea.

Any one can see the splendid even yellow of the
sugar maple or the sober scarlet of the red maple,
but it takes a trained eye to discover all the complexity of color that there is on the roadside in early
October, when the sky is clear and blue. The gray
birch and the white birch are turned a brilliant gold-

en yellow; the white trunks are spotted with palest of violet-blue shadows. The lichen-covered rocks in the stone wall are not gray, but green-gray of a sagey tone spotted with bits of brownish crimson. The beech bole is a mixture of pearly white and bluish gray, broadly spread with lilac shadows, and the leaves are the palest possible Naples yellow. The Virginia creeper (*Ampelopsis quinquefolia*) has turned not a pure crimson, but a deep, rich, cardinal red and maroon, and the berries with stems of coral-red are a misty cadet-blue. Everywhere the shadows on the roadside are bluish, and not a hint of black or neutral gray is visible. I can not prove this, of course, by bluntly asserting the fact, but I could demonstrate the truth of the statement by the aid of my paint-box and a bit of white paper. If we cut a small hole in the paper and at arm's length view the shadow through it we will certainly see the blue.

The full color of a tree or a mountain *can not be measured* if our attention is distracted by *details of form* which we see with remarkable ease. Subtility of color is not so readily perceived. It needs two pictures of the maple-lined road, one showing its June color and the other its October color, to prove that the light which shines in our faces and the shadow which lies ahead of us across the road are radically different in these two months because of the *change in color of the leaves.* Light on the country road is colored far more than we think it is, and as a natural consequence the shadows are colored.

I said that we saw details of form with astonishing ease, and that attention devoted to these prevented our seeing subtility of color. To prove this let me again suggest that we turn our heads upside down and look at the distant trees and mountains. I imagine that this will be the best way to wean our eyes from petty details, and show us a little more of the subtile color which is present in shadows, and the fire color which illumines autumn leaves; there is no mistaking the universal presence of it in Nature. Let me quote the testimony of Ruskin, who, at least the impressionist must acknowledge, misleads no one in the following statement about shadows: "Painters who have no eye for color have greatly confused and falsified the practice of art by the theory that shadow is an absence of color. Shadow is, on the contrary, necessary to the full presence of color, for every color is a diminished quantity or energy of light. And, practically, it follows from what I have just told you (that every light in a painting is a shadow to higher lights, and every shadow a light to lower shadows) that also every color in painting must be a shadow to

18

some brighter color, and a light to some darker one —all the while being a positive color itself." I am sure that the most thoughtful and considerate student of Nature must acknowledge her prodigal use of color nothing less than masterful. Where we least expect to find it there it lies in an amazing complexity of delicacy and strength. Landscape, flower, and bird are suffused with no end of it, and but rarely if ever show a hint of *true* black.*

In beast, bird, and fish, it is a curious and invariable fact that their underneath parts are extremely pale—almost white. Their safety is, in a great measure, dependent upon this lightened color which overcomes the shadow that must inevitably throw the creature into conspicuous relief, and thereby render its discovery by enemies the more probable. Not long since the artist Mr. Abbott Thayer, by a series of experiments with a number of objects painted light or dark beneath, demonstrated the fact that animals were greatly protected by their underneath light color. He proved that the object painted light beneath was lost to view much sooner than the one painted dark.

Color is a very active and important part of Na-

---

* Not even the crow is truly black. I have shown this in a previous chapter.

ture's plan in the preservation of life as well as the presentation of beauty. The gentle little grass-green snake (*Cyclophis vernalis*) glides harmlessly through the field unobserved except for the disturbance he creates among the weeds and grass leaves. Why he is not left alone it is hard to understand. No creature could possibly be more harmless. The cow-bird (*Molothrus ater*) is far more deserving of our animosity, for she lays her eggs in other birds' nests, and her young ones are the cause of the death of many an interesting brood. If people would only learn to let innocent snakes and toads live, we would have our farmers complaining less of destructive insects and worms. Poisonous snakes do not exist, so far as I know, among the White Mountains, and during the many seasons I have spent in the Catskills and at Lake George I have never met more than two rattlesnakes. It may be well enough to kill these and the treacherous copperheads, but the others should be allowed to live. Fully ninety per cent of the poor murdered reptiles I have seen by the roadside were perfectly harmless, and doubtlessly their loss was the gain of thousands of insects injurious to the farmers' crops.

The splendid color of the October landscape is æsthetic; that of snakes, butterflies, beetles, birds, and flowers is beautiful only as far as it is brilliant, or pure, or variegated. The atmosphere throws a veil of mystery over the hues of mountain, river, meadow, and tree in autumn, so that there is complexity in every tint. Every object is a mosaic of tiny colors, with a bit of purple here, orange there, and green yonder, as the case may be. But how is one to believe that, if color is so impalpable a thing that one must needs stand on one's head to see it? Well, there is no gain without pain. He who is told that a certain thing is extraordinary, must believe the fact until he *knows* the truth of it by self-acquired knowledge.

There is no short road to knowledge. If, by the wayside, we are unwilling to devote a great deal of time and attention to Nature, we must be content to travel blindly on without a taste of that broader, better life which in seeing and knowing possesses all things. The botanist, the entomologist, and the ornithologist are in possession of that greater knowledge of life which is equivalent to a power over all things. The impressionist has in his possession the key to Nature's mysteries of color. The power and the key are not beyond our reach.

INDEX.

261

THE END.

www.ingramcontent.com/pod-product-compliance
Lightning Source LLC
Chambersburg PA
CBHW021121270326
41929CB00009B/983